Pedestrian Road Safety Audit Guidelines and Prompt Lists

Making Your Roads Safer

FHWA-SA-07-007
July 2007

U.S. Department of Transportation
Federal Highway Administration

Technical Report Documentation Page

1. Report No. FHWA-SA-07-007	2. Government Accession No.	3. Recipient's Catalog No.
4. Title and Subtitle Pedestrian Road Safety Audit Guidelines and Prompt Lists		5. Report Date July 2007
		6. Performing Organization Code
7. Author(s) Dan Nabors, Margaret Gibbs, Laura Sandt, Sarah Rocchi, Eugene Wilson, and Martin Lipinski		8. Performing Organization Report No.
9. Performing Organization Name and Address Vanasse Hangen Brustlin, Inc. 8300 Boone Blvd., Suite 700 Vienna, VA 22182-2624		10. Work Unit No. (TRAIS)
		11. Contract or Grant No.
12. Sponsoring Agency Name and Address Federal Highway Administration Office of Safety 1200 New Jersey Ave., SE Washington, DC 20590		13. Type of Report and Period Covered Final Report 2-005-2007
		14. Sponsoring Agency Code

15. Supplementary Notes

This report was produced under the FHWA contract DTFH61-05-D-00024 , Technical Support for Office of Safety. The Task Manager was Gabe Rousseau (FHWA). Subcontractors were Opus Hamilton, Universtity of North Carolina Highway Safety Research Center, and PerformTech. The project team gratefully acknowledges the input provided by the technical working group over the course of this project. These individuals include: Sany Zein, Louisa Ward, Craig Allred, Michael Ronkin, Cara Seiderman, Barbara McMillen, Lois Thibault, and Richard Nassi. Significant contributions were also made by Charlie Zegeer, Daniel Rodriguez, Kelly Kennedy, David Anspacher, and Ryan Malloy. Report layout and design was performed by Michelle Scism of VHB.

The team also recognizes students who participated in an RSA workshop to help develop the prompt lists including Audrey Bowerman, Nicolas Estupinan, Carrie Fesperman, Ann Hartell, Anna Leos-Urbel, Peter Ohlms, and Jennifer Valentine.

16. Abstract

A road safety audit (RSA) is a formal safety examination of a future roadway plan or project or an in-service facility that is conducted by an independent, experienced multidisciplinary RSA team. All RSAs should include a review of pedestrian safety; however, some RSAs may be conducted to improve an identified pedestrian safety problem. The Pedestrian Road Safety Audit Guidelines and Prompt Lists provides transportation agencies and teams conducting an RSA with a better understanding of the needs of pedestrians of all abilities.

The Guide has two primary sections: Knowledge Base and the Field Manual. The Knowledge Base section discusses the basic concepts with which the RSA team should be familiar before conducting an RSA, such as understanding the characteristics of all pedestrians, analyzing pedestrian crash data, pedestrian considerations in the eight-step RSA process, and use of the Guide. The Field Manual section includes the guidelines and prompt lists. The guidelines provide detailed descriptions of potential pedestrian safety issues while the prompt lists are a general listing of potential pedestrian safety issues. The guidelines and prompt lists will help familiarize RSA teams with potential pedestrian issues and help them identify specific safety concerns related to pedestrian safety throughout the RSA process.

17. Key Words: pedestrian safety, road safety audits, engineering treatments		18. Distribution Statement No restrictions.		
19. Security Classif. (of this report) Unclassified	20. Security Classif. (of this page) Unclassified		21. No. of Pages 128	22. Price

Form DOT F 1700.7 (8-72)
Reproduction of form and completed page is authorized

Table of Contents

SUMMARY

A road safety audit (RSA) is a formal safety examination of a future roadway plan or project or an in-service facility that is conducted by an independent, experienced multidisciplinary RSA team. All RSAs should include a review of pedestrian safety; however, some RSAs may be conducted to improve an identified pedestrian safety problem.

The purpose of the *Pedestrian Road Safety Audit Guidelines and Prompt Lists* is to provide transportation agencies and RSA teams with a better understanding of the needs of pedestrians of all abilities when conducting an RSA. This pedestrian-specific guide presents a broad overview of the RSA process and how pedestrians should be considered in that process. The *FHWA Road Safety Audit Guidelines* (Publication FHWA-SA-06-06) should be referenced for more details on RSAs in general.

RSA teams should include safety experts with experience in developing the various aspects of a roadway and pedestrian facility. Expertise is needed to apply an understanding of pedestrian issues and their potential effects on pedestrian safety.

The Guide is divided into two primary sections: Knowledge Base and the Field Manual. An appendix providing supplemental information for RSAs is also included. The information provided and use of the primary sections in the conduct of an RSA is described in this summary.

The Knowledge Base section discusses the basic concepts with which the RSA team should be familiar before conducting an RSA, such as understanding pedestrian characteristics, pedestrian crashes, pedestrian considerations in the eight-step RSA process, and use of the Guide.

The Field Manual includes the guidelines and prompt lists. The guidelines provide detailed descriptions of potential pedestrian safety issues; the prompt lists are a general listing of potential pedestrian safety issues. The guidelines and prompt lists are designed to familiarize RSA teams with potential pedestrian issues and to help them identify specific safety concerns related to pedestrian safety throughout the RSA process. The guidelines and prompt lists are designed for RSA team members with varying levels of experience and skill sets; the more detailed guidelines may be useful to less-experienced RSA team members. RSA team members with more experience may find the less detailed prompt lists of more use.

The Guide provides two prompt lists: the master prompt list and the detailed prompt lists. The master prompt list (following page) presents the least detailed prompts and is the key to the Guide's organization. It is a general listing of safety topics by facility type. The detailed prompt list presents more specific issues to be considered. Appendix A provides both prompt lists.

The guidelines portion of the document (Chapter 5), present the most detailed description of the prompts. Illustrations and RSA examples provide a more detailed understanding of the potential issues that may be found during an RSA.

RSA Master Prompt List

Universal Considerations (For Entire RSA Site)	Topic	Subtopic	RSA Zones			
			A. Streets	B. Street Crossings	C. Parking Areas/Adjacent Developments	D. Transit Areas
I. Needs of Pedestrians: Do pedestrian facilities address the needs of all pedestrians? II. Connectivity and Convenience of Pedestrian Facilities: Are safe, continuous, and convenient paths provided along pedestrian routes throughout the study area? III. Traffic: Are design, posted, and operating traffic speeds compatible with pedestrian safety? IV. Behavior: Do pedestrians or motorists regularly misuse or ignore pedestrian facilities? V. Construction: Have the effects of construction on all pedestrians been addressed adequately? VI. School Presence: Is the safety of children in school zones adequately considered?	Pedestrian Facilities	1. Presence, Design, and Placement	Sidewalks, paths, ramps, and buffers	Crossing treatments, intersections	Sidewalks and paths	Seating, shelter, waiting/loading/ unloading areas
		2. Quality, Condition, and Obstructions	Sidewalks, paths, ramps, and buffers	Crossing treatments (see prompts in A)	Sidewalks and paths (see prompts in A)	Seating, shelter, waiting/loading/ unloading areas (see prompts in A)
		3. Continuity and Connectivity	Continuity/ Connectivity with other streets and crossings	Continuity/connectivity of crossing to ped network; channelization of peds to appropriate crossing points	Continuity/connectivity of pedestrian facilities through parking lots/adjacent developments	Connectivity of ped network to transit stops
		4. Lighting	Pedestrian lighting along the street	Lighting of crossing	Pedestrian level lighting in parking lots/adjacent developments (see prompts in A and B)	Lighting at and near transit stop
		5. Visibility	Visibility of all road users	Visibility of crossing/ waiting pedestrians and oncoming traffic	Visibility of pedestrians and backing/turning vehicles; visibility of pedestrian path	Visibility of pedestrians/ waiting passengers and vehicles/buses
	Traffic	6. Access Management	Driveway placement and design along streets	Driveway placement next to intersections	Driveway placement and use in relation to pedestrian paths	n/a*
		7. Traffic	Volume and speed of adjacent traffic, conflicting conditions	Volume and speed of traffic approaching crossing, conflicting movements	Traffic volume and speed in parking lots and developments, conflicting conditions	Volume and speed of adjacent traffic and traffic at crossings to bus stops, conflicting conditions
	Traffic Control Devices	8. Signs and Pavement Markings	Use and condition of signs, pavement markings, and route indicators	Use and condition of signs, pavement markings, and crossing indicators	Use and condition of signs, pavement markings for travel path and crossing	Use and condition of transit-related signs and pavement markings
		9. Signals	n/a*	Presence, condition, timing, and phasing of signals	n/a*	See prompts in B

Some of the topics in the matrix have listings that state "n.a." or "not applicable." This does not mean that there are no issues associated with a specific topic in a particular zone, rather there are no checks for the corresponding topic and RSA zone.

Chapter 1: INTRODUCTION

1.1 Purpose

The purpose of the *Pedestrian Road Safety Audit Guidelines and Prompt Lists* is to provide transportation agencies and road safety audit teams with a better understanding of the needs of pedestrians in the transportation system when conducting a road safety audit (RSA). An RSA is a formal safety examination of a future roadway plan or project or an existing facility, and is conducted by an independent, multidisciplinary team.

This document is an expansion of the pedestrian-related material in the *FHWA Road Safety Audit Guidelines* previously published by FHWA. The application of the RSA process outlined in these pedestrian-specific guidelines can assist agencies in better identifying the safety needs of pedestrians in their jurisdictions.

1.2 Scope of these Guidelines

The aforementioned *FHWA Road Safety Audit Guidelines* (Publication FHWA-SA-06-06, available online at http://safety.fhwa.dot.gov/rsa/rsaguidelines/html/documents/FHWA_SA_06_06.pdf) contains detailed information about the RSA process, how to implement an RSA program, as well as general prompt lists that show RSA review items for various project stages. This pedestrian-specific guide presents a broad overview of the RSA process and how pedestrians should be considered in that process. The *FHWA Road Safety Audit Guidelines* should be referenced for more details on RSAs in general.

The *Pedestrian Road Safety Audit Guidelines and Prompt Lists* (hereafter referred to as the Guide) presents RSA team members with issues they should consider when conducting a pedestrian RSA. While the authors have made every attempt to be as thorough as possible, persons performing RSAs are reminded that conditions vary from site to site and additional issues not documented herein may arise. That said, agencies should tailor prompt lists to their individual needs. Not all prompts included in this guide will be applicable for all areas. For example, the prompt "Will snow storage disrupt pedestrian access or visibility?" will not apply to all jurisdictions, and therefore should not be included as part of those areas' prompt lists.

RSA team members with an understanding of the RSA principles and process can use this publication to conduct an effective pedestrian oriented review of a facility. However, an RSA involving all modal facilities will require the use of both this guide and the *FHWA Road Safety Audit Guidelines*, with the pedestrian-specific guidelines helping the RSA team ensure that the pedestrian component of the RSA is adequately considered.

The focus of this guide is to help the RSA team identify potential pedestrian safety issues. It is not intended as a countermeasure selection guide. Other resources described in Section 1.7 and Appendix B provide state-of-the-practice information on selecting countermeasures.

1.3 Organization of the Guidelines

This guide is organized into several sections, including:

Knowledge Base

➤ Chapter 2: BASIC PRINCIPLES OF PEDESTRIAN SAFETY—provides an overview of the basic principles of pedestrian safety considerations, and where pedestrian issues are likely to occur.

➤ Chapter 3: PEDESTRIANS IN THE ROAD SAFETY AUDIT PROCESS—answers basic questions about conducting RSAs and how that process is applied to effectively assess and enhance pedestrian safety.

Field Manual

➤ Chapter 4: USING THE GUIDELINES AND RSA PROMPT LISTS—explains the structure of the prompt lists and field manual, and describes how to effectively use them when conducting a pedestrian safety audit.

➤ Chapter 5: DETAILED DESCRIPTIONS OF PROMPTS—presents the guidelines portion of the field manual, which provides detailed descriptions of the prompts, with examples of issues that may be encountered.

➤ Appendix A: PROMPT LISTS—contains the prompt lists to use when conducting an RSA.

Supplemental Information

➤ Appendix B: SUPPLEMENTAL INFORMATION—contains descriptions of other existing RSA tools and checklists that are used by various agencies.

The RSA Field Manual is the basic toolkit the RSA team will use when performing an RSA to include reviewing plans, conducting the field review, and writing the RSA report.

1.4 Background: Pedestrian Safety Risks

Walking is the oldest and most fundamental form of transportation, one that nearly every person uses on a daily basis. In fact, walking is not only a mode of travel in itself, but it is the mode that connects all other modes. Despite this, there remains a significant safety risk that detracts from the more widespread use and appeal of walking. In 2005, 4,881 pedestrians lost their lives and more than 64,000 were injured in the U.S. These figures may seem small in comparison to the number of motor vehicle occupant fatalities and injuries suffered each year (approximately 33,000 and 2,494,000, respectively) [1,2]. However, when exposure (i.e., the amount of time spent walking where there is potential of contact with a potentially harmful event) is taken into account, the relative risk by travel mode paints a far bleaker picture for pedestrians on a nationwide scale. The Surface Transportation Policy Project documented in a 2004 report that "although only 8.6 percent of all trips are made on foot, 11.4 percent of all traffic deaths are pedestrians"[3], underscoring the fact that pedestrians are among the most vulnerable users of the transportation system. The report also noted that in 2001—the last year all data were available—the fatality rate per 100 million miles traveled for pedestrians was more than 15 times higher for pedestrians than for motorists. Another study comparing fatality trends by mode—measured in terms of the number of deaths per 10 million hours traveled—reported that "the nationwide fatality rate for 2001 is estimated to be 4.94 deaths per 10 million hours for walking and 2.90 deaths per 10 million hours for motoring" [4]. Regardless of whether exposure is measured by distance traveled or by time spent traveling, the evidence is clear that the pedestrian mode of travel faces significantly more risk relative to motor vehicle travel.

1.5 Addressing Pedestrian Safety

Increasing Pedestrian Infrastructure Investments

Highway agencies, decision makers, and developers are recognizing the importance of considering pedestrians in transportation projects and investing in appropriate infrastructure. Many agencies are establishing goals and objectives that focus on increasing usage of alternative modes, such as walking, as well as improving safety and connectivity for these modes. As a result, transportation and land use planning initiatives, and infill development, are often explicitly considering pedestrian infrastructure requirements in addition to roadway improvements.

This shift in emphasis is further illustrated by the language in FHWA policy calling for the routine inclusion of pedestrians and bicyclists in all projects. This has led to increasing emphasis on pedestrians in the latest editions of nationally accepted engineering publications, such as the *Manual on Uniform Traffic Control Devices* (MUTCD). More documents that focus on pedestrians have been developed as well, such as the *AASHTO Design Guide for Pedestrians* (2004). Additionally, the federal government has made positive steps toward supporting more pedestrian transportation investments.

Improving Understanding of Pedestrian Issues through RSAs

Increases in pedestrian facility investment by developers and local, state, and federal transportation agencies are certainly helping to address safety issues and reduce pedestrian risks. However, even with the support provided by governments, national guidelines, and local and regional plans, many agencies and localities still have a difficult time knowing how to approach inclusion of pedestrians in their transportation plans and improvement projects. RSAs are a cost effective method to proactively identify safety issues and make suggestions on measures and facilities to improve pedestrian safety.

1.6 Road Safety Audits

An RSA is a formal safety examination of an existing or future roadway that is conducted by an independent, multidisciplinary team. By "independent," it is meant that the RSA team will not be the same as the party charged with the development of the original plans or the facility owner. (The term "owner" will be used throughout this document to refer to the person or agency that owns or is responsible for the project). If a person associated closely with the development of a project or plan (i.e., not an independent auditor) wishes to review and evaluate the pedestrian safety elements of a project, it is still a valuable process but not a formal RSA. See the *FHWA Road Safety Audit Guidelines*, Section 3.2, for a description of various types of design and construction review processes.

RSA Objectives

The main objective of an RSA is to address the safe operation of roadways and crossings to ensure a high level of safety for all road users. The RSA can be conducted at any stage of a project, from the project planning stage to the final design stage, or on existing projects, though earlier in the project process there are more opportunities for effective and efficient solutions to safety concerns. Conducting an RSA on an existing facility represents a major portion of the roadway network where pedestrian safety can be retroactively improved, given that many older projects have not been designed with adequate consideration of the needs of pedestrians or where pedestrian use has increased since construction.

> RSAs are not intended to be a review of design standards or policies, but rather a review of site elements that, alone or combined, could contribute to safety concerns.

The Evolution of RSAs

RSAs have been used for decades to examine the safety of a future or existing roadway, and much information is available on conducting RSAs. The recent *Road Safety Audit Guidelines* provides the knowledge base for starting an RSA program in various agencies. RSA guidelines and prompt lists (sometimes known as checklists) have been created and employed by a variety of agencies in the U.S. and abroad, most notably Canada and Australia. These guidelines often provide detailed information about current RSA processes, the objectives of these tools, the parties responsible for implementing them, and major issues to consider in the RSA. However, many of the RSA documents already available cover the RSA process and contain only high level information about technical topics. Given that many traffic engineers have little training or experience in determining pedestrian safety needs and methods to safely accommodate pedestrians of all abilities, the needs of pedestrians may not be explicitly or adequately considered in transportation projects or in RSAs. Nearly all transportation projects have some degree of pedestrian activity, even those in rural areas, where pedestrians may face a higher risk because they are less expected by drivers. These factors make it critical to develop tools to assist RSA teams in identifying potential pedestrian safety issues and suggesting countermeasures.

Accordingly, this document and companion prompt list are intended to provide skilled safety practitioners with the necessary tools to identify pedestrian safety issues in an RSA.

1.7 Knowledge Base for Conducting RSAs

Before conducting RSAs, it is critical that RSA team members have a working knowledge of pedestrian design requirements as well as an understanding of the relative safety various design features may provide. The following sections outline national standards, guidelines, and safety resources that are important for the RSA team to understand. This list of materials is by no means comprehensive, but the RSA team should be aware of the content of these resources as a minimum before conducting an RSA. This will help the RSA team members check for conditions where combinations of minimum standards may render a facility difficult or hazardous for pedestrians, especially

> RSA teams should include safety experts with experience in developing the various aspects of a roadway and pedestrian facility. For example, at least one person on the team should be familiar with the Americans with Disabilities Act (ADA) requirements so as to understand how these affect design options, and how safety concerns for all road users can be addressed while meeting the ADA requirements.

those with limited sensory and mobility abilities, or under challenging conditions (such as night or high vehicle speeds).

Standards

The RSA team should be familiar with national and State guidelines and standards when conducting an RSA. These standards are covered in:

> *AASHTO A Policy on Geometric Design of Highways and Streets* (Green Book) https://bookstore.transportation.org/item_details.aspx?ID=110

> *ADA Accessibility Guidelines (ADAAG)* http://www.access-board.gov/adaag/html/adaag.htm

> *Manual on Uniform Traffic Control Devices (MUTCD)* http://mutcd.fhwa.dot.gov/ser-pubs.htm

> Applicable State-specific documentation, such as State statutes and laws governing pedestrian and motorist responsibilities

The ADAAG describes minimum designs of elements providing accessibility for pedestrian use. The ADAAG is a minimum design standard (the starting foundation), however, not a best practice document. Many situations require additional measures to ensure safety, especially in high use areas as well as situations where pedestrian travel is not anticipated by motorists in suburban and rural areas.

Best Practices

An understanding of best practices of pedestrian facilities is also necessary. Guidance on recommended practices is described in:

> *FHWA Designing Sidewalks and Trails for Access, Part I, A Review of Existing Guidelines* http://www.fhwa.dot.gov/environment/sidewalks/

> *FHWA Designing Sidewalks and Trails for Access Part II, Best Practices Guide* http://www.fhwa.dot.gov/environment/sidewalk2/

> *FHWA Accessible Sidewalks and Street Crossings - An Informational Guide (FHWA-SA-03-019)* http://www.bikewalk.org/pdfs/sopada_fhwa.pdf

> *AASHTO Guide for the Planning, Design, and Operation of Pedestrian Facilities* https://bookstore.transportation.org/item_details.aspx?id=119

> *AASHTO Guide for the Development of Bicycle Facilities* https://bookstore.transportation.org/Item_details.aspx?id=104 These documents and tools provide valuable information about potential countermeasures that can mitigate pedestrian safety concerns for an audited roadway or facility.

Safety Resources

Documents

➤ *A Guide for Reducing Collisions Involving Pedestrians (NCHRP Report 500)*
http://onlinepubs.trb.org/onlinepubs/nchrp/nchrp_rpt_500v10.pdf

➤ *Safety Effects of Marked Versus Unmarked Crosswalks at Uncontrolled Locations (HRT-04-100)* http://www.tfhrc.gov/safety/pubs/04100/index.htm

➤ *How to Develop a Pedestrian Safety Action Plan (FHWA-SA-05-12)*
http://www.walkinginfo.org/pp/howtoguide2006.pdf

➤ *Improving Pedestrian Safety at Unsignalized Crossings (NCHRP Report 562)*
http://onlinepubs.trb.org/onlinepubs/nchrp/nchrp_rpt_562.pdf

➤ *Road Safety Audits: Case Studies (FHWA-SA-06-17)*

Tools

➤ PEDSAFE: The Pedestrian Safety Guide and Countermeasure Selection System (FHWA-SA-04-003) http://www.walkinginfo.org/pedsafe/

➤ Pedestrian and Bicycle Crash Analysis Tool (PBCAT)
http://www.bicyclinginfo.org/bc/pbcat.cfm

The documents and tools listed above should be used in concert with the safety resources during project planning and design. Facility design and operations are affected by one another, as is safety, and a change in either aspect of a facility could have an effect on safety.

Chapter 2: BASIC PRINCIPLES OF PEDESTRIAN SAFETY

This chapter provides a brief background and synthesis of pedestrian safety principles that RSA teams need to understand in order to better evaluate the pedestrian environment and improve the quality and safety of facilities that support the pedestrian mode of travel.

2.1 Walking as a Mode of Travel

Although it is frequently under-accounted for in transportation planning models and processes, walking remains a major mode of transportation. Trips made primarily by walking (based on 2001 National Household Transportation Survey data) account for between 6 and 16 percent of all trips[5]. While walking is often a recreational activity, a large portion of walking trips are "utilitarian," and include travel made for work, education, and shopping purposes.

Walking is also an important connector between different travel modes. While some trips are made entirely by walking, others may involve walking as only one component of a trip, such as walking to catch a bus to school, walking from home to the car on the way to work, or walking from a vehicle parked in a lot to the grocery store. Walking trips to transit or between modes are typically not counted as walking trips, but are included in part of trips made by other modes. Hence, walking trips may be underrepresented, and pedestrians' exposure to risk may be higher than can be assumed from transportation surveys. As such, there is a need to accommodate pedestrians safely and to provide access and mobility at all types of transportation facilities.

2.1.1 Factors that Influence the Decision to Walk

The decision to walk is usually based on a complex interaction of factors, including but not limited to some of the following:

> **Distance and Access to Desired Destinations**—Many factors affect walking distance and access such as land use patterns, and directness of pedestrian facilities, connectivity of the sidewalk network, and the presence of barriers to walking. Locations with high density and mixed land uses can reduce trip distances by providing a variety of destinations within a compact area. Road networks based on a grid—with short blocks and intersections that facilitate pedestrian crossing—provide more opportunities for direct and fast pedestrian connections to destinations. Areas where pedestrian facilities do not provide direct access to destinations or where there are critical gaps discourage walking.

> **Necessity**—Voorhees states "walking remains the cheapest form of transport for all people, and the construction of a pedestrian-friendly environment provides the most affordable transportation system any community can plan, design, construct, and maintain.[6]" Eight percent of Americans live in a home without access to a car [7], and even in households with vehicle access, there are people without the ability to drive due to age, limited financial resources, medical conditions, or other factors.

> **Safety and Comfort**—Actual and perceived safety concerns can influence the decision and ability of people to walk, including high traffic speeds, lack of separation from vehicular traffic, inadequate walking and crossing facilities, and time. Low speeds, wide walkways that are separated from traffic traveling at low speeds, large numbers

of pedestrians, and well-lit spaces tend to encourage walking by providing a greater sense of safety and security.

> **Health**—Just as a health condition can limit a person's ability to drive, it can also limit the ability to walk. At the same time, walking may be chosen by some road users as a form of exercise having substantial health benefits.

> **Weather**—Inclement weather can not only affect a person's decision to walk, it can affect the path they choose to take. Pedestrian facilities not resistant to changes in weather can cause pedestrians to take paths that may conflict with vehicular and bicycle traffic.

2.1.2 Barriers to Walking

Physical, social and perceptual, and organizational issues may discourage people from walking:

> **Physical Barriers**—These consist of unprotected street crossings, lengthy crossings, crossings that are spaced too far apart, interchanges, partial or nonexistent walking paths, poor quality walking surfaces, nonexistent or inappropriate crossing treatments, and high speed traffic.

> **Social and Perceptual Barriers**—These include a perception that motorists disregard or are uninformed of pedestrian rights, that walking is a risk to personal safety, or that there is insufficient time to make a walking trip.

> **Organizational Barriers**—These make walking more difficult by affecting decisions that influence the ease of a walk, including land use patterns that result in long trip distances, greater priority given to other modes (such as at intersections), and lack of recognition of the importance of providing pedestrian facilities.

The RSA team should understand these factors that influence people's decisions to walk and the barriers they may face if and when they decide to walk. A clear understanding of these concepts can help the RSA team better identify these barriers through the RSA process and to be able to suggest changes that can effectively reduce or eliminate such barriers and improve pedestrian safety.

2.2 Pedestrian Characteristics

Pedestrians have a wide range of characteristics and needs, such as walking speed, spatial needs, mobility issues, and cognitive abilities. However, facilities for a "typical" pedestrian may not accommodate a significant portion of users, including older adults, people with disabilities, and children. It is crucial to understand the characteristics of the full range of the pedestrian population that may use the facilities to ensure the design of pedestrian facilities accommodates the range of pedestrian abilities.

> **Walking Speed**—While the average pedestrian walks at about four feet per second, many older adults, children, and people with mobility impairments walk more slowly. Pedestrian crossing times at signalized intersections and available gaps at unsignalized intersections must take into account the presence of slower walkers.

> **Spatial Needs**—Where sidewalks and crosswalks cannot accommodate high

pedestrian volumes, pedestrian traffic may move very slowly or some people may walk in the street. Even in less crowded areas, street furniture or landscaping may reduce the sidewalk space available for pedestrians. Since walking is often a social activity, many pedestrians traveling in groups will walk in the street or along the grass in order to stay side by side. Pedestrians using wheelchairs require additional space to navigate sidewalks. Work zones may not adequately provide for the spatial needs of pedestrians, especially those with disabilities.

➤ **Mobility**—Many pedestrians, especially young children, people with disabilities, and some older adults, have lower mobility levels. They also may have reduced motor skills that limit their ability to walk at certain speeds, turn their heads in certain ways, and see all signs, signals, and markings. Young children or people in wheelchairs may be less visible because of their lower height and in turn may not be able to see some vehicles.

➤ **Vision**—Pedestrians with limited vision may be the group at the largest disadvantage on the road network, as vision is needed to perceive nearly all communication and cues from the roadway environment. Age-related vision loss is a common cause of low vision and blindness, and with the cohort of older Americans growing rapidly, limited vision will continue to increase as a pedestrian safety concern.

➤ **Cognitive Abilities**—Many pedestrians, particularly children under 12 years old, may not have the developmental ability or experience to judge vehicle speed and distance accurately. Road users of any age may be temporarily impaired by illness, drugs, or alcohol. Pedestrians, like drivers and other road users, do not always give full attention to the traffic environment, or may be distracted.

➤ **Crossing Choices and Waiting Times**— Pedestrians usually prefer to travel in the most direct route possible. If blocks are excessively long, or if crossings do not provide safe and accessible routes that directly connect the destinations people want to reach, many pedestrians will walk or cross outside the provided pedestrian infrastructure. Similarly, pedestrians who must wait for an excessive amount of time to cross a street (some studies have found that more than 30 seconds is too long) may walk against a pedestrian signal or cross at another location.

Other pedestrian characteristics include the ability or likelihood of changing direction quickly or unexpectedly (especially children). This, along with lighting, affects the ability of motorists to see the pedestrian and have sufficient time to react to pedestrian movements. The RSA team should always keep in mind these types of pedestrian characteristics when performing an RSA and consider how they would be affected by various conditions and influence the safety of the pedestrian environment.

2.3 Factors that Contribute to Pedestrian Crashes

As mentioned in the introduction to this guide, pedestrian crashes with motor vehicles are a major cause of highway injuries and fatalities each year. Yet, it is likely that pedestrian crashes are still vastly underreported[8] due to crashes that occur in non-roadway locations (such as on private property or shared use paths) and the number of crashes that do not involve police. Various behavioral, location, and physical conditions that contribute to a pedestrian crash can often be determined from historical crash records. This section describes these conditions of which an RSA team should be aware when conducting an RSA.

2.3.1 Behavioral Crash Factors

Driver and pedestrian behaviors are coded in crash reports to help understand events that contributed to a crash. Driver behaviors include failure to yield right of way, driving too fast, and inattention to name a few; pedestrian behaviors include, but are not limited to, improper crossing, failure to yield right of way, and darting into the road. There have been many studies that have looked at behavioral typing of crashes to gain a better understanding of potentially hazardous behaviors of both drivers and pedestrians. However, behavioral crash factors derived from crash reports may be misleading as many jurisdictions cite pedestrian behaviors as a contributing factor to a crash without considering the facilities afforded to pedestrians. A classic example is where a pedestrian struck by a vehicle while crossing an intersection is found to have been crossing improperly, yet there are no pedestrian signal heads at the intersection.

2.3.2 Location Factors

It is important for the RSA team to have an understanding of locations where pedestrian crashes may occur. Several studies have attempted to analyze pedestrian crash data in an attempt to determine locations where pedestrians are at the highest risk. A 1995 FHWA study identified and analyzed locations related to pedestrian fatal and injury crashes[9]. The study developed fifteen major sub groups of pedestrian crash types, as shown in Table 1. The crash types listed in Table 1 are organized in order of most common crash type subgroups (such as intersection crashes where drivers violated a traffic law). The highlighted rows in the table group intersection-related and midblock related crashes to demonstrate the relative occurrence of pedestrian crashes at intersection and midblock locations. There are four general areas where a crash can take place:

1. At an intersection (where pedestrian is crossing).
2. At a midblock location (where pedestrian is crossing).
3. Along the road (where pedestrian is not trying to cross).
4. Not in the roadway.

In terms of location, almost one-third of the crashes studied occurred within 50 feet of an intersection. Collisions with turning vehicles and "other" intersection incidents were the most prevalent intersection-related crashes (62 percent of intersection-related crashes). Another 7.2 percent of all crashes (or 22 percent of intersection-related crashes) occurred due to an intersection dash—when the driver's view of the pedestrian was impeded until just before the crash or when the pedestrian was running. In addition, 5.1 percent of all crashes (16 percent of intersection-related crashes) occurred due to a driver violation at an intersection.

Midblock crashes were the second largest subgroup of pedestrian crashes, accounting for almost 27 percent of all pedestrian crashes. The most prevalent type of midblock crash was the midblock dash, in which a pedestrian crossed the road and the driver's view was not blocked, but the driver may not have had time to stop. Midblock darts occur when the motorist's view was obstructed until just before impact with the pedestrian. Midblock dart/dashes crashes accounted for nearly 14 percent of all crashes.

Other, more recent studies and reports on pedestrian crashes have reported similar locational trends to the ones above[10]. Knowledge of these studies may help the RSA team assess the relative risks of walking by location and ensure that potential safety concerns in all areas are addressed.

Table 1: Percent of Crashes by
Major Pedestrian Crash Type Subgroups[9]

Pedestrian Crash Type Subgroup	Percent of Pedestrian Crashes
Midblock dart/dash	13.3
Other midblock	13.2
Other intersection	10.1
Vehicle turning at intersection	9.8
Not in road	8.6
Walking along roadway	7.9
Miscellaneous	7.8
Intersection dash	7.2
Backing vehicle	6.9
Driver violation at intersection	5.1
Working/playing in roadway	3.0
Disabled vehicle related	2.4
Driverless vehicle	2.1
Other vehicle-specific	1.9
Bus-related	0.9

Midblock-related   **Intersection-related**

2.3.3 Physical Crash Factors

The physical qualities of the roadway and pedestrian network may affect pedestrian safety. Below are some characteristics of the travel network that should be considered in an RSA:

- ➤ **Vehicle Speed**—The geometric design of streets may allow drivers to feel comfortable at higher speeds than originally intended. Though pedestrian fatalities occur when vehicle speeds are low, increased speed increases the likelihood of severe injuries and fatalities if struck. In addition, high speeds increase the potential of other roadway environment factors, such as low skid resistance, contributing to crashes.

- ➤ **System Connectivity** (or lack of a system altogether)—While the volumes of pedestrians in rural, suburban, and urban areas can differ substantially, it is important to provide pedestrian provisions in all environments where pedestrians will or will likely be using the roadway. Pedestrian activity may make it necessary to provide sidewalks along both sides of the road. Potential conflicts between pedestrians and vehicles may necessitate providing marked crosswalks and other treatments at intersections. All pedestrian facilities should be continuous, consistent, and connected along direct routes to major pedestrian traffic generators. Urban designs with short blocks and high densities tend to support pedestrian connectivity better than rural areas. People in rural areas tend to rely more on the automobile for mobility than those in urban areas. While this leads to fewer potential conflicts between vehicles and pedestrians, it reduces motorist expectation of encountering pedestrians at intersections and driveways or walking along the side of the road. While it may not be feasible to provide a sidewalk along a rural road, some basic pedestrian provisions, such as a walkable shoulder, should be provided.

➤ **Crossings**—Compared to motorists, pedestrians are often exposed to greater risks of injury, and risks increase in relationship to motor vehicle speeds. The challenge is to protect pedestrians where they are most vulnerable—at roadway crossings. Each time a pedestrian crosses a street, there is a potential conflict with traffic. These conflicts can be the result of legal traffic movements, such as permissive left turns and right turns on red. They can also be the result of illegal movements such as running a red light or crossing against a walk signal.

➤ **Transit Stop Placement**—Since much pedestrian traffic is generated by bus passengers traveling to and from bus stops, these crossing locations deserve additional considerations and coordination among transit and highway agencies. A well-planned transportation network can use intersection elements (e.g., crossing distance and signal timing) to reduce the potential conflicts while accommodating all modes.

➤ **Access Management**—Vehicles turning into and out of driveways will conflict with pedestrians walking along roadways, presenting opportunities for crashes. These conflicts can be reduced by consideration of pedestrians during the planning stages of a project, and by consolidating existing driveways. Driveways close to intersections, in addition to the safety risks they present to vehicular traffic, can increase the workload on pedestrians that have to focus their attention on traffic from multiple directions.

2.4   Using Crash Data for an RSA

For an RSA of an existing facility, crash data may be available. Crash data can be used to identify locations where there are safety concerns; however, it may not be possible to determine any consistent pattern in pedestrian crashes as reported pedestrian crashes tend to be rare. Therefore, more than three years crash data may be needed to see any trends. Even then an area may have few pedestrian crashes because few pedestrians choose to walk, especially those whose modal choices are more limited – older people, people who have vision and cognitive impairments, and children.

When apparently reliable crash data are available, the RSA team should consider the data carefully, and try to determine if land use and other roadway characteristics have changed. This is more difficult to do when dealing with pedestrian crashes as pedestrian traffic can change drastically without any evidence of roadway changes. For example, store closings can drastically affect pedestrian traffic, relocation of bus stops, and many other events that are difficult to determine. Furthermore, as described in Section 2.3.1, assessments of fault should be carefully reviewed in crash reports, since fault is often inappropriately assigned to pedestrians regardless of conditions.

The RSA team should fully understand these data constraints, realizing that a review of crash data alone is generally not sufficient to comprehensively identify and address pedestrian safety issues. A thorough understanding of pedestrian safety issues requires a site visit as described in more detail in Section 3.5.

Chapter 3: PEDESTRIANS IN THE ROAD SAFETY AUDIT PROCESS

This section provides the user with detailed information pertaining to pedestrians in the RSA process. More detailed information about RSAs, to include creating RSA policies and procedures and generalized prompt lists, are included in the *FHWA Road Safety Audit Guidelines* released in 2006.

3.1 What is an RSA?

As described in Chapter 1, an RSA is a formal safety examination of a future roadway plan or project or an in-service facility that is conducted by an independent, experienced multidisciplinary RSA team.

The primary focus of an RSA is safety (as opposed to mobility, access, aesthetics, etc.), although other aspects are considered. The intent of an RSA is to consider the potential safety issues of all users under all conditions. The RSA may be applied to any type of facility and can examine the potential safety issues for any type of road, throughout the project development process, and on completed facilities.

The RSA is not a simple standards check. Standards checks are part of the design process to ensure adherence to standards and guidelines. Although the RSA team may identify safety issues by comparing items of concern to standards, it is generally done with the intention of identifying areas where combinations of minimum standards may interact with road user behaviors to generate a potential safety issue.

The RSA team has no mandate to change a design that is being audited. The RSA team is charged with reviewing a project to identify its safety implications, and suggesting measures (for the design team's or responsible agency's consideration) that can reasonably be implemented within the project schedule and available budget.

3.2 What Should be Audited?

In addition to using the traditional RSA as a tool to improve safety performance of facilities under their jurisdiction, public agencies may wish to conduct *pedestrian-oriented RSAs*. Though all RSAs could include a review of pedestrian and bicycle safety, a pedestrian-oriented RSA may be undertaken to improve an identified pedestrian safety problem which may have resulted from inadequate consideration of pedestrian needs in the planning and design process.

A pedestrian-oriented RSA may also be conducted on projects in the planning or design stage. Examples of projects with a substantial pedestrian component include projects near significant pedestrian generators, such as transit stations, multi-family housing, schools, school bus stops, assisted living facilities, or in a downtown area or commercial district. Other areas that may benefit from an RSA include:

> Work zones.

> Arterial streets.

> Off-street paths (including walkways or pedestrian/bicycle bridges).

While the focus of a pedestrian-oriented RSA is to identify pedestrian safety concerns, it still considers the safety of all modes, especially how they relate to each other. When one mode is given preference over another, safety issues often arise. The tools in this guide are designed to be used in both traditional and pedestrian-oriented RSAs.

3.3 Who Should Conduct RSAs?

An increasing number of state departments of transportation (DOTs) are using RSAs as a proactive tool for improving safety. Many pedestrian issues occur on arterial roadways which are typically owned by state DOTs. This guide can be used by state DOTs to help ensure pedestrian safety is integrated into the RSA process.

Pedestrian safety is a major concern for many local agencies and as such, they may find a greater need for conducting a pedestrian-oriented RSA. The challenge is to assemble an independent team given the staffing limitations of most local agencies. Since independence is a requirement of an RSA, the local agency should contact the state DOT, the Local Technical Assistance Program (LTAP) center, the FHWA division office, or the FHWA resource center for assistance in finding team members. The local agency may also find it helpful to contact adjacent local agencies directly to put together an independent team; however they must ensure that the team has adequate training and experience. Considerations for the RSA team responsibilities, skills, and size are discussed in Section 3.5 of this report.

More detailed information on how a local agency can assemble an RSA team can be found in NCHRP Synthesis 321, Roadway Safety Tools for Local Agencies.

3.4 When Should RSAs be Conducted?

RSAs can be conducted at any one of several stages of a project: Pre-construction (planning, preliminary design, final design); Construction (work zone traffic control plan, pre-opening); and Post-construction (existing roads open to traffic). Agencies should strive to start an RSA at the earliest feasible stage of a project. An RSA in the early stages of planning and design can identify issues when they can most easily be rectified. RSAs on existing projects are helpful in identifying pedestrian safety issues in that many agencies devote less resources to understanding pedestrian issues and therefore may be unaware of problems or may not be experienced with detailed pedestrian facility design. It is a common perception that public officials may think a pedestrian problem may not exist based on a review of pedestrian crashes. However, as discussed in Section 2.3, we know that many pedestrian crashes go unreported, or there are no pedestrian crashes because there are no pedestrians and no pedestrian facilities. RSAs can help agencies better understand pedestrian issues in their jurisdiction.

RSAs conducted on new pedestrian facilities during or after the construction stage can evaluate the effectiveness of permanent and temporary traffic control devices.

3.5 How is an RSA Conducted?

The typical eight steps followed in conducting an RSA at any stage of a project are described in this section. Suggestions for ensuring pedestrians are adequately considered in this process are provided.

	Typical 8 RSA Steps	Responsibilities	
		Project Owner/ Design Team	RSA Team
Step 1	Identify project or existing road for RSA	✔	
Step 2	Select multi-diciplinary RSA team	✔	
Step 3	Conduct start-up meeting to exchange information	✔	✔
Step 4	Perform field reviews under various conditions		✔
Step 5	Conduct RSA analysis and prepare report of findings		✔
Step 6	Present RSA findings to Project Owner / Design Team	✔	✔
Step 7	Prepare formal response	✔	
Step 8	Incorporate findings into project when appropriate	✔	

The responsibilities of the project owner/design team and the RSA team vary during the course of an RSA.

Step 1: Identify Project or Existing Road for RSA

The project owner identifies the project(s) to be audited. The owner should develop clear parameters for the RSA. The parameters should define the RSA scope, schedule for completion, RSA team requirements, required tasks and requirements on the content and format of the RSA report, and how responses to the RSA report will be handled.

Step 2: Select Multi-diciplinary RSA Team

The project owner is responsible for selecting the RSA team or the RSA team leader. The RSA team must be independent of the project being audited. The RSA team's independence assures that there is no potential conflict of interest and a fair and unbiased evaluation will be conducted. The project owner may select a set of qualified individuals from within its own organization, another road authority, or hire an outside group. If a consultant is selected to conduct the RSA, the project owner may want to also provide input into the desired RSA team skills.

The project owner should also ensure that the RSA team represents a group of individuals that, combined, possess a set of skills that will ensure the most critical aspects of the project are addressed. RSA team members should have a background in road safety, traffic operations and/or road design. For RSAs with a significant pedestrian component and in particular, pedestrian-oriented RSAs, a pedestrian specialist should be included on the RSA team. A pedestrian specialist's insight and knowledge will assist the RSA team with identifying issues that are not obvious to team members having general or other areas of expertise. Ideally, the pedestrian specialist will have experience in planning and designing pedestrian facilities, and will have formal training on accessibility and pedestrian-specific design. Individuals representing other specialty areas, such as transit operations, enforcement, and emergency-response personnel may be aware of constraints and problems that affect pedestrians. Persons with independent local knowledge from neighborhood pedestrian organizations may also provide valuable insights into potential safety issues affecting pedestrians.

The size of the RSA team may vary. While three members may be adequate for some projects, that number may not be sufficient for larger, more complex projects. The best practice is to have the smallest team that brings all the necessary knowledge and experience to the process.

Step 3: Conduct Start-up Meeting to Exchange Information

The purpose of the pre-audit meeting is to:

> ➤ Hand over all relevant data, information, and drawings to the RSA team.
> ➤ Review the scope and objectives of the RSA.
> ➤ Delegate responsibilities.
> ➤ Agree upon a schedule for the completion of the RSA.
> ➤ Set up lines of communication between the RSA team leader, the project owner, and the design team.
> ➤ Communicate matters of importance to the RSA team.

If possible, the project owner/design team should provide data describing pedestrians such as pedestrian crash data, pedestrian traffic volumes, peak and off peak hours of pedestrian travel, locations of key pedestrian generators, and citizen requests and complaints. The design team should inform the RSA team of design constraints, standards used, results of previous RSAs, and any issues arising, if applicable. The RSA team must also be aware of local traffic laws, statutes, and customary usage affecting pedestrians. The design and operation of pedestrian facilities should be consistent with local laws and customs governing issues such as pedestrians in unmarked crosswalks. At the end of the meeting, all parties should have a clear understanding of the scope of the RSA to be undertaken and each of their roles and responsibilities.

Step 4: Perform Field Reviews Under Various Conditions

Design drawings and other project information should be reviewed prior to and after the field review. Field reviews should be conducted for each RSA stage and type of RSA but are particularly useful in post-construction or RSAs of existing facilities. During the site visit, members of the RSA team should review the entire site, noting issues. Issues identified in the review of project data should be verified in the field.

A thorough site review for an RSA with a significant pedestrian component will include the following actions as a minimum:

The field review is a key task in the RSA process.

> ➤ **Include a walk-through.** The RSA team should include both daytime and night-time observations to experience conditions from not only the perspective of a pedestrian, but from all other roadway users. This is very important in identifying elements that may increase the risk of collision for pedestrians. Ideally, the RSA team will walk the most traveled pedestrian paths

and note potential issues in not only facility design, but also pedestrian behavior and behavior of other modes. The field review should also include visits during both peak and non-peak traffic conditions. Pedestrian safety, mobility, and access are heavily influenced by traffic conditions and different issues may be present under different traffic conditions.

➤ **Consider a wide range of pedestrian abilities.** A wide range of pedestrian experience and capabilities must be accommodated. Pedestrian designs should accommodate child pedestrians who lack experience and development judging vehicles and safe gaps for crossing, as well as adults with differing hearing, vision, cognitive, and mobility levels.

➤ **Consider visibility of pedestrians, especially at night.** Pedestrians may enter the road at locations when drivers are focused on other tasks. Pedestrians may also have very limited visibility relative to motor vehicles, especially at night. These factors increase the risk of collision, especially in situations where drivers are watching for

potentially conflicting vehicles, such as where right-turns-on-red are permitted at channelized right turn lanes. Where risk factors are identified, measures to increase motorists' visibility of pedestrians, or reduce motor vehicle speeds on the approach to conflict points, may be beneficial.

➤ **Examine the treatment and transition of pedestrian facilities at the project limits.** Pedestrian facilities should be designed with attention to connecting facilities at the project limits and during construction. Discontinuities in facilities can result in pedestrians being forced to share the road with vehicles, exposing them to increased risk of collisions. It is also important to become aware of pedestrian and driver behaviors beyond the project limits. Designs outside of the project limits may have a significant

The median pictured above seems to adequately protect pedestrians from through traffic. However, review of the same site at night reveals that there are in fact safety concerns for pedestrians in the crosswalk. Street lighting is blocked by trees, which may reduce visibility of pedestrians in the crosswalk, especially to vehicles turning left from the side street (not pictured, to the right of the photo).

effect on pedestrian and driver behavior. An example of this is a traffic calming project that diverts cut-through traffic from a neighborhood, increasing the volume on main streets. If this volume leads to congestion, it could increase frustration of both drivers and pedestrians.

The Field Manual, consisting of the prompt list instructions (Chapter 4), the guidelines (Chapter 5), and the prompt lists (Appendix A) are designed to be used during the field review to remind the RSA team to look at all aspects of pedestrian safety. This is done by the RSA team reviewing the prompt lists in the field for each type of pedestrian facility encountered and annotating any issues on paper. A more detailed description of the organization of the guidelines and prompt lists and how to use them is provided in Chapter 4.

Step 5: Conduct RSA Analysis and Prepare Report of Findings

The RSA team prepares an analysis of the safety issues identified based on the field visit and the review of documents. Prior to preparing a report, the team may meet with the project owner/design team to discuss preliminary findings. The purpose of this meeting is to establish a basis for writing the RSA report and to insure that the report will address issues that are within the scope of the RSA process.

The RSA report is a concise document, typically only a few pages in length. It should include a brief description of the project, a listing of the RSA team members and their qualifications, a listing of the materials used in conducting the RSA and a summary of findings/suggestions. It should include pictures and diagrams that may be useful to further illustrate points made. The Field Manual will help the RSA team prepare the RSA report to ensure all points are covered. RSA examples are provided as an illustration of how problems can be identified and how suggestions can be made.

Often the RSA report may include a crash risk assessment of each issue which can be used to identify a priority. This assessment is based on the expected crash frequency and the expected severity of a crash. Expected crash frequency is qualitatively estimated on the basis of expected exposure (how many road users will likely be exposed to the identified safety issue) and probability (how likely is it that a collision will result from the identified issue). Expected crash severity is qualitatively estimated on the basis of factors such as anticipated speeds, expected collision types, and the likelihood that vulnerable road users will be exposed. These two risk elements (frequency and severity) are then combined to obtain a qualitative risk assessment on the basis of the matrix shown in Table 2.

Speed greatly affects the severity of the crash when a pedestrian is involved. At 40 mph, there is an 85 percent chance of a pedestrian fatality; the fatality rate drops to 45 percent at 30 mph, at 20 mph the fatality rate is only 5 percent[11]. Based on these data, it is clear that vehicular collisions involving pedestrians will tend to have higher severity ratings than for vehicular-only collisions, typically in the serious to fatal range. This type of qualitative rating scheme underscores the vulnerability of pedestrians, but it is not the only rating method that can be applied. It is up to the RSA team to agree upon an assessment method suitable to the purposes of the RSA being conducted. The method should consider the relationship between speed and severity described above.

Table 2. Crash Risk Assessment

FREQUENCY RATING	SEVERITY RATING			
	Minor	*Moderate*	*Serious*	*Fatal*
Frequent	Moderate-High	High	Highest	Highest
Occasional	Moderate	Moderate-High	High	Highest
Infrequent	Low	Moderate	Moderate-High	High
Rare	Lowest	Low	Moderate	Moderate-High

Step 6: Present RSA Findings to Project Owner/Design Team

The RSA team presents the results of the RSA to the project owner/design team. This is a further opportunity for discussion and clarification and the project owner/design team may wish the RSA team to present additional detailed information on the RSA findings.

Step 7: Prepare Formal Response

Once the project owner and the design team have reviewed the RSA report, they should jointly prepare a written response to its findings. The response should outline what actions the project owner and/or design team will take to each safety concern listed in the RSA report. A letter report format, signed by the project owner, is a valid method of responding to the RSA report. Since pedestrian issues typically have a high degree of public involvement, particularly at the local level, presenting the RSA findings in a public meeting or making the report available to the public may help garner support for the RSA process and the RSA findings.

Step 8: Incorporate Findings into the Project when Appropriate

After the response report is prepared, the project owner/design team implements the agreed-upon safety improvements or creates and documents a plan for implementation of the safety improvements. An important consideration is to develop a program to evaluate the RSA program and share 'lessons learned' within the organization.

3.6 Anticipated Challenges in Conducting Pedestrian-Oriented RSAs

While the number of agencies implementing RSA programs is increasing, there are numerous challenges faced by organizations to achieve the full integration of RSAs in their pedestrian safety programs. The following are some of the key challenges:

> **Identifying the projects that are prime candidates to be audited.** In many cases, the issue of pedestrian safety is not given a high priority—for example, on building construction projects that close sidewalks. Procedures need to be established that ensure that pedestrian issues are addressed in all projects. Using the RSA for those projects that are identified as having a significant impact on pedestrian flows can potentially have major benefits. Refer to Section 3.4 for additional information on the types of projects for which pedestrian RSAs should be considered.

> **Using the RSA process at schools.** Schools pose unique pedestrian safety problems because of the age of pedestrians and the mix of pedestrian, bicycle, and vehicular traffic. Potential issues are exacerbated with the increasing number of students driven to school, thereby increasing the number of drop-off and pick-up points. Because of the uniqueness and complexity of a school's problems, a review by an independent RSA team helps assure that a balanced approach is taken to address safety. School officials and parents are closely involved with the problems and are acutely aware of day-to-day operation of the school facility and have strong opinions regarding problems and their solutions. The value of the RSA team's findings is in the independent perspective of the task and the need to consider a variety of stakeholder viewpoints and perceptions in the process.

➤ **Convincing agencies of the need for an independent, experienced auditor on pedestrian focused projects.** Many communities have been conducting RSAs or similar environmental assessments with untrained or informal auditors such as community members. While local community members who often use the facilities being audited have a strong awareness of many problems observed on those facilities, they may not have the background knowledge necessary to identify relationships to the built environment and potential solutions. Another problem with local community members using the RSA is that they may be used to certain situations and not perceive them as threatening and potentially risky as an outside trained auditor might; "fresh eyes" may be needed to take into consideration a variety of safety concerns and provide innovative recommendations to mitigate issues. Although outside RSA team members may not have an institutional memory of the facilities being audited, they may 1) carry less bias in terms of considering safety issues, 2) be better trained to comprehensively assess the environment and identify relationships between safety, behavior, and the physical and social environment, and 3) be in a better position to coordinate findings with the responsible parties to promote change and implement improvements.

➤ **Ensuring the needs of all roadway users are considered.** Whereas the focus of this guide and materials is on pedestrians, it is paramount that the needs of all users are considered when conducting an RSA. This includes not only understanding design principles, but also the laws that affect all users. Failure to consider all users appropriately may result in potential safety issues going unnoticed by the RSA team or inappropriate suggestions being made for all road users. For example, installation of a sign or signal for one type of user may create sight distance issues for another type. The intent of this guide is to assist RSA teams in considering potential pedestrian issues, not to lead teams to place any lower priority on other road users.

➤ **Understanding the different relationships between agencies and the public in pedestrian-oriented RSAs.** Pedestrian-oriented RSAs may involve local pedestrian and community groups either as part of the RSA team, or as advocates for specific issues or concerns. Members of these groups may be able to add more details on the pedestrian's perspective of facilities, thus further ensuring the needs of users are met. Sometimes an RSA may even be initiated at the request of such a group. It is important for the RSA team to consider the role these organizations may play in the improvement process when planning an RSA and suggesting mitigation strategies.

Many pedestrian issues, such as closing a driveway to reduce pedestrian-vehicle conflicts, require local agencies to work with private land owners.

Chapter 4: USING THE GUIDELINES AND RSA PROMPT LISTS

4.1 Purpose of the Guidelines and Prompt Lists

The intent of both the guidelines and prompt lists is to familiarize RSA teams with potential pedestrian issues and to help them identify specific safety concerns related to pedestrian safety. The prompt list is a useful tool to help RSA teams identify the range of design, operational, and policy elements that may affect pedestrian safety. Users should not rely on the prompt list as a simple yes/no checklist. It is a tool to "prompt" their thoughts and judgment when looking at a road user characteristics, design issues, environmental factors, and policies affecting pedestrian safety. The prompt lists may not cover all issues affecting pedestrian safety, and experienced team members can contribute to the success of RSAs. The prompt lists are not a product of an RSA, rather they are a means by which that product can be created. Findings from the RSA should always be described in an RSA report as discussed in Section 3.5.

4.2 Organization of the Guidelines and Prompt Lists

The guidelines (Chapter 5) and prompt lists (Appendix A) are designed for RSA team members with varying levels of experience and skill sets. The guidelines and prompt lists have different levels of detail to meet the needs of the users different skill levels. The hierarchical structure of these tools, shown in increasing levels of detail, is as follows:

1. Master Prompt List.
2. Detailed Prompt List.
3. Guidelines.

The master prompt list presents the least detailed prompts. It is a general listing of topics while the detailed prompt lists presents more specific issues that need to be considered. The master prompt list serves as an index for guidelines and prompt lists, also called the Field Manual. The master prompt list consists of two basic elements: the universal considerations and the matrix of pedestrian prompts (see Figure 1). The RSA matrix consists of 3 major topic areas, 9 subtopic categories and 4 RSA zones. Typically, RSA teams will review the prompts in all 9 subtopic categories for each RSA zone encountered during the RSA.

RSA Master Prompt List

Universal Considerations (For Entire RSA Site)	Topic	Subtopic	A. Streets	B. Street Crossings	C. Parking Areas/Adjacent Developments	D. Transit Areas
I. Needs of Pedestrians: Do pedestrian facilities address the needs of all pedestrians?	Pedestrian Facilities	1. Presence, Design, and Placement	Sidewalks, paths, ramps, and buffers	Crossing treatments, intersections	Sidewalks and paths	Seating, shelter, waiting/loading/unloading areas
II. Connectivity and Convenience of Pedestrian Facilities: Are safe, continuous, and convenient paths provided along pedestrian routes throughout the study area?		2. Quality, Condition, and Obstructions	Sidewalks, paths, ramps, and buffers	Crossing treatments (see prompts in A)	Sidewalks and paths (see prompts in A)	Seating, shelter, waiting/loading/unloading areas (see prompts in A)
III. Traffic: Are design, posted, and operating traffic speeds compatible with pedestrian safety?		3. Continuity and Connectivity	Continuity/Connectivity with other streets and crossings	Continuity/connectivity of crossing to ped network; channelization of peds to appropriate crossing points	Continuity/connectivity of pedestrian facilities through parking lots/adjacent developments	Connectivity of ped network to transit stops
IV. Behavior: Do pedestrians or motorists regularly misuse or ignore pedestrian facilities?		4. Lighting	Pedestrian lighting along the street	Lighting of crossing	Pedestrian level lighting in parking lots/adjacent developments (see prompts in A and B)	Lighting at and near transit stop
V. Construction: Have the effects of construction on all pedestrians been addressed adequately?		5. Visibility	Visibility of all road users	Visibility of crossing/waiting pedestrians and oncoming traffic	Visibility of pedestrians and backing/turning vehicles; visibility of pedestrian path	Visibility of pedestrians/waiting passengers and vehicles/buses
VI. School Presence: Is the safety of children in school zones adequately considered?	Traffic	6. Access Management	Driveway placement and design along streets	Driveway placement next to intersections	Driveway placement and use in relation to pedestrian paths	n/a*
		7. Traffic	Volume and speed of adjacent traffic, conflicting conditions	Volume and speed of traffic approaching crossing, conflicting movements	Traffic volume and speed in parking lots and developments, conflicting conditions	Volume and speed of adjacent traffic and traffic at crossings to bus stops, conflicting conditions
	Traffic Control Devices	8. Signs and Pavement Markings	Use and condition of signs, pavement markings, and route indicators	Use and condition of signs, pavement markings, and crossing indicators	Use and condition of signs, pavement markings for travel path and crossing	Use and condition of transit-related signs and pavement markings
		9. Signals	n/a*	Presence, condition, timing, and phasing of signals	n/a*	See prompts in B

The RSA team should familiarize itself with the prompts so that they understand that there is a certain degree of cross checking required between zones and topics on the RSA matrix. For example, if auditing a parking area/adjacent development, RSA teams should understand that they need to not only check RSA Zone "C: Parking Area/Adjacent Development", but also "A" for any streets on-site, "B" for street crossings, and "D" for transit accessing the site.

Some of the topics in the matrix have listings that state "n.a." or "not applicable." This does not mean that there are no issues associated with a specific topic in a particular zone, rather there are no checks for the corresponding topic and RSA zone.

Figure 1. Pedestrian RSA Master Prompt List

The master prompt list (i.e., both the universal considerations and the RSA matrix) of pedestrian prompts are potential issues that should be considered at all times when conducting an RSA. They apply to the RSA area as a whole and how the system of pedestrian facilities interfaces with other transportation components.

Detailed descriptions of the universal considerations are included in the guidelines. The RSA matrix has a more detailed prompt list in Appendix A and a detailed explanation of the prompts in the guidelines. The detailed prompts are referenced from the RSA matrix by RSA zone (column), identified with a letter A-D, and the subtopic area (row), identified by a number 1-9. For example, the RSA matrix in Figure 1 shows in that lighting (4) on streets (A) should be investigated by the RSA team during the RSA. More detailed description of the prompt is provided in the detailed prompt list and is referenced by the code A.4. Likewise, the most detailed explanation of these prompts for this category can be found in the guidelines (Chapter 5) under A.4. Figure 2 shows an explanation of the detailed prompt lists.

B. Street Crossings

The master prompts are a general listing of topics that the RSA team should consider. These make up the RSA matrix and apply to the audit area as a whole and how the system of pedestrian facilities interact with other transportation components. A master prompt should be checked for all RSA stages. An experienced RSA team may be able to use only the master prompt list.

The detailed prompt list presents more detailed concerning specific issues or characteristics. A discussion of each is found in the guidelines (Chapter 5).

Some detailed prompts are the same across different pedestrian zones and are referenced in the matrix and detailed prompt list.

Master Prompt	Detailed Prompt	planning	design	construction	post-construction
	B.1.1 Do wide curb radii lengthen pedestrian crossing distances and encourage high-speed right turns?		✓	✓	✓
	B.1.2 Do channelized right turn lanes minimize conflicts with pedestrians?	✓	✓	✓	✓
	B.1.3 Does a skewed intersection direct drivers' focus away from crossing pedestrians?	✓	✓	✓	✓
	B.1.4 Are pedestrian crossings located in areas where sight distance may be a problem?	✓	✓	✓	✓
B.1 Presence, Design, and Placement	B.1.5 Do raised medians provide a safe waiting area (refuge) for pedestrians?	✓	✓	✓	✓
	B.1.6 Are supervised crossings adequately staffed by qualified crossing guards?		✓	✓	✓
	B.1.7 Are marked crosswalks wide enough?		✓	✓	✓
	B.1.8 Do at-grade railroad crossings accommodate pedestrians safely?		✓	✓	✓
	B.1.9 Are crosswalks sited along pedestrian desire lines?	✓	✓	✓	✓
	B.1.10 Are corners and curb ramps appropriately planned and designed at each approach to the crossing?		✓	✓	✓
	See prompts in Section A for potential issues on obstructions and protruding objects that apply to street crossings				
B.2 Quality, Condition, and Obstructions	B.2.1 Is the crossing pavement adequate and well maintained?				✓

RSA Stages

Figure 2. Detailed Prompt List Format (excerpt from Appendix A)

The Field Manual parallels the prompt list and provides a more detailed explanation of the potential issues that may arise. Each prompt has a more detailed explanation and often examples of areas of concern that help illustrate potential issues.

4.3 When to Use the Guidelines and Prompt Lists

The pedestrian guidelines and prompt lists can be used as part of all RSAs for all projects with a pedestrian component. Pedestrians are often road users for projects, whether facilities are designed accordingly. For this reason, the RSA team should anticipate that pedestrians will be users of the project they are auditing even if they are not the primary focus. The pedestrian needs identified in the prompt lists will help to ensure adequate consideration of pedestrian safety issues. The RSA team can use the prompt lists during:

> ➤ The review of project information and design drawings.
> ➤ Field reviews and site visits.
> ➤ Review of RSA results and suggestion development.
> ➤ Report writing.

The detailed prompt list indicates the stage of project which the prompts need to be considered. Generally, all items on the master prompt list should be checked for all RSA stages. The level of information and design details increases as projects become more defined. Projects in the planning or preliminary design stages are less detailed, with the result that the RSA team addresses only general pedestrian issues (such as whether sidewalks or pedestrian signals will be provided). As the design progresses, more detail is available in the design drawings, so the RSA should include more detailed considerations (such as actual sidewalk width or the adequacy of pedestrian signal timings). For RSAs of existing facilities, the RSA team must consider these same detailed considerations, as well as review the condition of existing pedestrian infrastructure (such as the condition of the sidewalk, or whether accessible pedestrian signal heads are correctly oriented, operating properly and adequately maintained). These levels of detail have been accommodated in the prompt lists in this document.

4.4 How to Use the Guidelines and Prompt Lists

The prompt lists and guidelines are designed to accommodate RSA team members with varying degrees of experience in pedestrian safety issues. Inexperienced RSA team members can find detailed descriptions of safety issues in the guidelines section (Chapter 5). RSA team members with slightly more experience may choose to use only the detailed prompt list. RSA team members with even more experience may focus on the master prompt list. Very experienced RSA team members may choose to use a combination of the master prompt list and the category and subcategory columns of the master prompt list (these reflect the prompts which have the least detail). Before conducting an RSA, all RSA teams should familiarize themselves with the prompt lists and guidelines.

As RSA team members become more familiar with pedestrians issues, the safety issues associated with the guidelines and prompt lists will become an accepted practice in ensuring that the RSA does not overlook important safety issues. RSA team members using the prompt lists for the first time will want to thoroughly review the detailed prompt list and guidelines; after several uses they will have a better understanding of the detailed issues and be able to use the general prompt list to remind themselves of the facility characteristics that need to be checked.

The RSA team is reminded that these prompt lists are intended to provide guidance to help the RSA team address pedestrian safety. The prompt lists are not checklists that provide a simple listing of all pedestrian items to be considered in an RSA. For this reason, the RSA team should not use the prompt lists as a checklist, either in the RSA process or in the RSA report. Rather, the prompt lists are provided to identify the types of pedestrian-related issues that the RSA team should be aware of to promote pedestrian safety in the audited project. It is the responsibility of the RSA team to address pedestrian safety in a realistic and thoughtful manner, using the prompt lists as a guide to help them address the potentially wide range of pedestrian issues.

Chapter 5: GUIDELINES – DETAILED DESCRIPTIONS OF PROMPTS

This section provides information to help users understand the underlying issues that the questions in the prompt lists bring up and be able to better identify concerns during the RSA process. The descriptions will help the RSA team gain a more detailed understanding of conditions and other issues that are likely to affect pedestrian safety. The structure of this section parallels that of the prompt lists. The guidelines are divided into five parts:

➤ **Universal Considerations**—describes potential issues that need to be considered throughout the study area at all times regardless of the type of facility being reviewed or observed.

➤ **Streets (Section A)**—describes potential issues on sidewalks, trails, or any path that may be used by pedestrians.

➤ **Street Crossings (Section B)**—describes potential issues on a pedestrian facility that crosses a facility for another mode of travel such as intersections or rail crossings.

➤ **Parking Areas/Adjacent Developments (Section C)**—describes potential issues at areas outside of the public right of way that may have safety issues or influence pedestrian and driver behavior on the public right of way. Many of the issues that are outside of the public right of way are covered in the Streets and Street Crossings sections; however, more detailed site specific issues are covered in this section.

➤ **Transit Areas (Section D)**—identifies potential issues specific to transit locations (i.e., bus stops and light rail stops), emphasizing issues at bus stops (e.g., the mode most used and where most problems exist).

At the beginning of each section is a brief overview and a discussion of terms used in the section. The numbering of the detailed descriptions of prompts in this section corresponds to the numbering of the actual prompts in the prompt lists in Appendix A. This will enable the RSA team to easily relate the prompt list items to the guidelines.

The guidelines will help an RSA team gain a better understanding of what to look for when conducting an RSA at any stage of a project. The RSA team is cautioned, however, that issues may arise that are unique to a specific area and that may not be covered in the guide—the guidelines are not exhaustive. Furthermore, the prompts that are included in this document should not be used as a "yes or no" checklist. The RSA team is also reminded to review the prompts in similar or overlapping areas. For example, pedestrian issues at driveways are described in *Section A: Streets* and *Section C: Parking Areas/Adjacent Developments*. References to such similar areas are included in the detailed description of the prompts.

Guidance in this section is provided in two formats:

➤ Detailed description of prompt.
➤ RSA Examples.

The detailed descriptions of the prompt may include the following:

> ➤ Problem description to include situations where issues arise and potential specific consequences.
> ➤ Special considerations for the RSA team.
> ➤ Photographs illustrating the problem.

The RSA examples serve to further illustrate issues as they may be described in an RSA report. The structure of the examples is presented below:

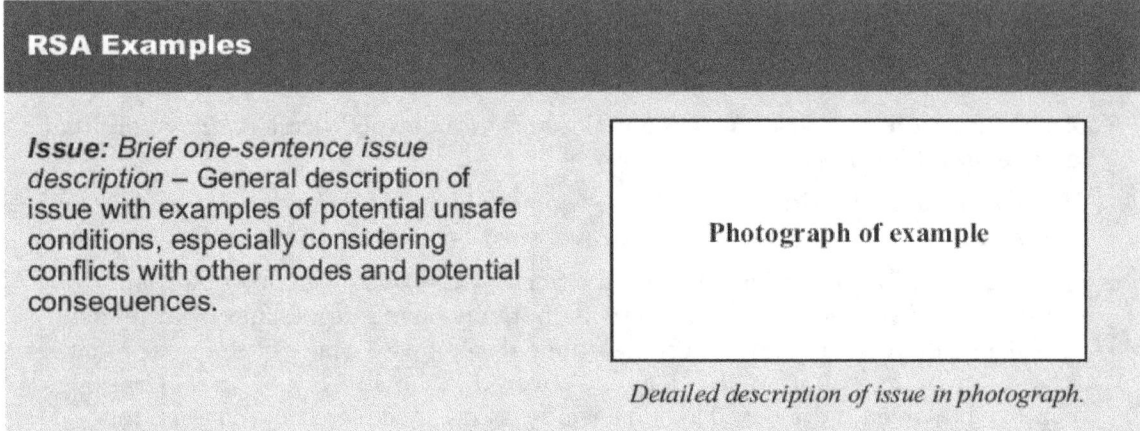

RSA Examples

Issue: *Brief one-sentence issue description* – General description of issue with examples of potential unsafe conditions, especially considering conflicts with other modes and potential consequences.

Photograph of example

Detailed description of issue in photograph.

The RSA examples will contain more site-specific information than can be found in the descriptions in the detailed prompts.

UNIVERSAL CONSIDERATIONS

Overview

Unlike the prompts in Sections A-D, which are intended to be considered when auditing specific areas of the pedestrian network, the prompts in this section should be considered throughout the entire RSA area regardless of the project stage. These "universal" prompts are not location specific and should influence every consideration of pedestrian safety. For example, the potential issues prompted by the question "Do pedestrian facilities address the needs of all pedestrians?" (Prompt 1) should be considered at all times and for all areas that the RSA covers. The Universal Considerations prompts are included in the master prompt list.

Terminology used in this section:

Pedestrian "desire lines" are the preferred paths of pedestrians in a roadway network. Pedestrian desire lines often trace the shortest or most convenient paths between two points or more specifically, significant pedestrian generators. One sign that pedestrian facilities are needed is the presence of worn paths (though the absence of a worn path does not necessarily mean that a sidewalk or path is not needed).

I. Needs of Pedestrians: Do pedestrian facilities address the needs of all pedestrians?

Pedestrians can vary greatly in their abilities, as described in Chapter 2. The RSA team should consider whether pedestrian facilities are designed to take into account all user groups. The RSA team should determine if there is a predominance of a particular user group due to the presence of facilities such as hospitals, schools, parks, and multi-modal centers (including airports, rail stations, intercity bus terminals, and water ports), since pedestrians associated with these facilities may have specific needs that may not be adequately accommodated by the application of minimum standards alone.

> *Seniors* may walk more slowly than other adult pedestrians and therefore may need more time at crossings. Are sufficient gaps in the traffic available, or are pedestrian signals timed, to allow slower pedestrians to safely cross?

> *Children* have a limited ability to recognize danger, may be more impulsive in their movements, and are often more difficult for motorists to view because of their height. Are there obstructions that would prevent a driver from seeing a child at and approaching intersections and driveways? How are facilities perceived by a young child?

> *People in wheelchairs, scooters, with strollers or dollies* require curb ramps, continuous, smooth surfaces, and sufficient space to operate and wait. Where these are not provided, they may find it necessary to travel in the street or may be delayed when clearing a crosswalk. Are curb ramps that line up with crosswalks

The level landings for each of these ramps on this refuge island do not connect, making it difficult for pedestrians with vision or mobility restrictions.

provided? Do curb ramps on islands or other refuge areas line up with each other?

➤ *People with visual impairments* may need tactile or audio cues to warn them of upcoming conflict points or obstructions. Are these cues provided at appropriate locations?

➤ *Non-English speaking* pedestrians and children may not be able to read or understand text or complex signing. Do signs convey a simple, clear meaning?

II. Connectivity and Convenience of Pedestrian Facilities: Are safe, continuous, and convenient paths provided along pedestrian routes throughout the study area?

The "connectivity" of a pedestrian network describes the continuous nature of a network that is free of gaps or obstacles. An example of good connectivity would be a marked pedestrian crosswalk connecting two sidewalks, with well-positioned curb ramps to allow wheeled pedestrians to stay entirely within the bounds of the sidewalks and crosswalk at the transition between them.

The "convenience" of a pedestrian network describes the qualities that make it comfortable and easy to use. Some characteristics of a pedestrian network that contribute to its convenience include its geometry (for example, flat grades), its passability under all weather conditions, and how directly it follows pedestrian desire lines.

Inconvenient or poorly connected pedestrian facilities can cause pedestrians to choose alternative routes, which may put them into conflict with vehicles and cyclists. The RSA team should evaluate the convenience and connectivity of the pedestrian network within and at the limits of the RSA area, and consider areas where connectivity and convenience are often deficient:

➤ Interchanges in urban areas.

➤ Private developments, especially those where buildings are separated from the street by parking facilities (see Section C).

➤ Large arterial roadways.

An adequate number of crossings should be provided for all pedestrians. Crossings should take into account the abilities, speeds, and other behavioral characteristics of pedestrians and should meet pedestrian demands and desire lines.

RSA Example

Continuity: *The pedestrian network should be continuous for all users.* A continuous walkable surface that is accessible to all users, including those with limited mobility and vision, promotes the use of the pedestrian network and helps keep pedestrians out of roadways, where they may conflict with cyclists and vehicles.

A paved sidewalk (foreground) transitions to an unpaved footpath in an urban area. Pedestrian volumes are significant along the footpath, which serves a bus stop. The footpath may be impassable for all users when wet or icy, and provides an uneven surface that may render it difficult for pedestrians with low vision, in wheelchairs, or pushing strollers. The RSA team may suggest installing an adequate sidewalk.

III. Traffic: Are design, posted, and operating traffic speeds compatible with pedestrian safety?

High traffic speeds can increase the risk and severity of a pedestrian collision, as well as make the pedestrian environment less attractive. As described in Chapter 2, research has shown speed has a significant impact on mortality rates in collisions between pedestrians and motor vehicles. The RSA team should consider traffic speeds and their effect on pedestrian safety on all RSAs.

IV. Behavior: Do pedestrians or motorists regularly misuse or ignore the pedestrian facilities?

The RSA team should observe if pedestrians or motorists are misusing or ignoring pedestrian facilities. Typically, this will point to the presence of other issues. For both design-stage RSAs and RSAs of existing facilities, the RSA team should assess whether existing pedestrian facilities follow pedestrian desire lines. For RSAs of existing facilities, the RSA team should also consider the following questions:

- ➤ Do pedestrians cross at uncontrolled locations because marked or controlled crossings are dangerous, inconvenient, or not placed appropriately?
- ➤ Do pedestrians disobey pedestrian channelization devices and signage intended to prohibit travel by foot in specific areas?
- ➤ Do motorists observe traffic control devices (e.g., signals, stop signs, etc.)?
- ➤ Do motorists look for and yield to pedestrians at crossings?

V. Construction: Have the effects of construction on all pedestrians been addressed adequately?

Construction or reconstruction of roads, pedestrian facilities, buildings, or other developments may affect pedestrian safety. Pedestrians of all ability levels should have continuous pedestrian routes through or around the construction area. Pedestrian routes should be separated from traffic, clearly marked, signed, and lighted, and adequately maintained. Specifically, the RSA team should investigate the following:

> ➤ Are designated pedestrian detour routes provided, and are they separated from traffic and clearly marked and/or signed?

> ➤ Are detour routes free from adverse environmental effects (e.g., mud, water, etc.) and adequately lighted for night-time use?

> ➤ Are detour routes part of a continuous network of pedestrian facilities?

> ➤ Are detour routes, alternate routes, and temporary pedestrian routes accessible to pedestrians with all abilities (e.g., are stable curb ramps provided)?

Pedestrian paths should be continuous, even during periods of construction. In the photo above, an alternate accessible path around construction has not been provided, leaving a gap in the sidewalk.

Inappropriate signage and channelization fails to effectively convey safe travel paths for pedestrians. In the photo above, the wrong signing fails to direct pedestrians to the proposer crossing.

A good example of a temporary curb ramp is one made of a stable material such as asphalt or concrete, not sand or wood.

VI. School Presence: Is the safety of children in school zones adequately considered?

Schools often generate a significant amount of pedestrian activity by children, especially schools located in residential areas. Children walking to and from school share the road environment with school buses and private vehicles picking up or dropping off students. The visibility, practical experience, and physical and mental capabilities of child pedestrians are substantially different from those of adults, requiring the RSA team to consider the functionality and safety of pedestrian facilities from a child's perspective. The RSA team should consider the following:

- ➤ Are pedestrian facilities adequate in the area surrounding the school (e.g., do sidewalk widths accommodate peak periods of pedestrian traffic)?
- ➤ Is pedestrian signing near schools adequate and effective?
- ➤ Do pedestrian facilities provide connectivity to residential areas or transit facilities?
- ➤ For children that take the bus, do sidewalks provide direct access from the bus loading area for the school, without crossing parking lots or traffic lanes?
- ➤ Are drop-off/pickup lanes separated from bus lanes to minimize confusion and conflicts?
- ➤ Are school gates appropriately located to provide convenient and direct access for pedestrians?
- ➤ Are crossings in school zones marked as school crossings?

A. STREETS

Overview

The prompts in this section are intended to help the RSA team identify pedestrian safety problems along streets.

To promote a safe environment for walking, pedestrians must be provided space to walk along the public right of way. Pedestrian pathways can take many forms. In urban and suburban areas where pedestrian volumes may be high, sidewalks are typically the most appropriate facility. In rural areas, where pedestrian traffic might be less frequent, walkable shoulders may be sufficient. Trails or shared-use paths can safely convey pedestrians along parkways.

Pedestrian facilities should provide accessible, safe, and continuous links to adjacent destinations regardless of facility type. Missing segments in the pedestrian network can leave pedestrians stranded, cause pedestrians to travel in the street, and increase conflicts between pedestrians and other modes. Without a continuous and connected pedestrian network, pedestrians are more likely to walk in the street and cross the street at unexpected points, such as at midblock locations. Furthermore, pedestrian sidewalks and paths should be as direct as possible, built along pedestrian "desire lines" that provide direct access to major origin and destination points.

This section of the guidebook provides a more detailed description of the prompts for pedestrian safety along streets. The section numbers correspond to the numbered prompt lists.

> **Terminology used in this section:**
>
> *Sidewalks*–Sidewalks are formal pedestrian facilities located adjacent to a roadway. They can be paved (such as concrete, asphalt, or brick) or unpaved surfaces that are maintained. Informal gravel/dirt pathways (also referred to as "goat trails") that are not maintained are not considered sidewalks since they may not provide the safest route for pedestrians.
>
> *Trails and shared-use paths*– Trails and shared-use paths can be important pedestrian linkages. Many of the concerns for sidewalks are also concerns for trails, meaning that many of the prompts in this section can be used to conduct an RSA on a trail. However, the RSA team may wish to consult publications that specifically discuss trail design to better assess trail safety issues.
>
> *Buffers*–A buffer is a linear space provided between the sidewalk and the road to help separate pedestrians from other road users, especially motor vehicles.

A.1 Presence, Design, and Placement

A.1.1 Are sidewalks provided along the street?

Sidewalks are the primary facility type for pedestrians along streets. As such, **the presence of sidewalks is one of the primary considerations for the RSA team**. Failure to provide adequate sidewalks, or another adequate facility (see prompt A.1.2), increases exposure of pedestrians walking along the road to other travel modes using the roadway.

On existing streets, sidewalks may not be provided because of inadequate right of way. This may occur on existing streets with low volumes of pedestrians where the road has grown to fill the available right of way. Sidewalks may also be missing in rural communities, often adjacent to rural highways. These potential challenges should be understood and addressed by the RSA team.

A.1.2 If no sidewalk is present, is there a walkable shoulder (e.g. wide enough to accommodate cyclists/pedestrians) on the road or other pathway/trail nearby?

Streets without sidewalks can adequately accommodate pedestrians if there is sufficient space outside the vehicle travel lanes. These "walkable" shoulders should be paved and are often found along rural roads where there are few pedestrians.

If a walkable shoulder is present, the RSA team should also consider the following:

- ➤ Are shoulders wide enough to accommodate pedestrian and bicycle volumes, considering pedestrians of all abilities (prompt A.1.4)?
- ➤ Are shoulders continuous and provide links to other pedestrian facilities?
- ➤ Are shoulders adequately maintained (i.e., free of mud, severe pavement deterioration, and plowed snow)?
- ➤ Are shoulders clearly delineated by clear and well-maintained pavement markings?

Photo by Michael Ronkin

The photo on the left shows a walkable shoulder. The safety of this shoulder, especially for children, may be a concern depending upon vehicular traffic volume, composition, and speed, pedestrian volume and composition, bicycle traffic, and the presence of lighting. The photo on the right shows a walkable shoulder which is separated from traffic by a wide pavement marking stripe. This wide stripe appears to offer a wider buffer between pedestrian and vehicular traffic. However, the safety of this shoulder may be a concern if it is frequently used by children since they may not always exhibit the safest behavior. As the photo illustrates, these children are walking with their backs to the traffic, which is not the recommended practice. Shoulders should not be relied upon as the only pedestrian facility near a school.

If neither a sidewalk nor a walkable shoulder is present, a nearby parallel trail or shared-use path may be present. If such a facility is present, the RSA team should determine the adequacy of this facility in connecting pedestrians to nearby land uses.

A.1.3 Are shoulders/sidewalks provided on both sides of bridges?

Narrow bridge structures (including structures which constrain the width of the roadway, such as tunnels or culverts) are common problem areas for pedestrians in both urban and rural environments. The best time to incorporate pedestrian facilities on bridges is before bridge construction is completed. During the planning and design stage of a project it is important to ensure that walkable paths are provided on both sides of the bridge and that the width is adequate to accommodate both existing and future pedestrian volumes.

Underestimating current or future pedestrian volumes on bridges may result in inadequate walking facilities on existing bridges. Since bridge expansions are costly, measures to widen travel lanes may be made at the expense of the pedestrian facilities. As a result, pedestrian pathways may be provided on one side of the bridge only. While such a design can be made to accommodate pedestrians, the RSA team should assess the connectivity of pedestrian links to the bridge. Pedestrians crossing the street at or near the ends of the bridge are undesirable, not only because driver and pedestrian expectancy is violated, but because the bridge structure may obstruct sight lines between drivers and pedestrians.

The photo on the left shows pedestrians walking along an unpaved shoulder where no sidewalk or paved pathway is provided. The narrow shoulder at a culvert forces pedestrians to walk in the road. The photo on the right shows a bridge that has been retrofitted with exclusive pedestrian and bike lanes.

A.1.4 Is the sidewalk width adequate for pedestrian volumes?

Minimum widths specified in the ADAAG are often inadequate to meet the needs of pedestrians. When large groups of pedestrians are present on the sidewalk, and sufficient space is not provided, pedestrian traffic will move slowly, causing some people to walk in the street, or cross to the other side of the street, violating driver expectancy. Even in less crowded areas, pedestrians may walk in the street if the sidewalk is not wide enough, or they may decide to cross the street at an unsafe location to reach a sidewalk with less traffic. Since walking is often a social activity, many pedestrians traveling in pairs or groups will walk in the street or along the grass in order to stay side by side with others.

The RSA team should determine if the width of the usable sidewalk is adequate to meet pedestrian volumes. The RSA team should observe peak pedestrian volumes that are specific to certain times of day (such as school-related peaks), certain days of the week (such as near a sports field used on the weekends), or certain times of the year (such as near a seasonal vendor area, park, or "university" town). On planning or design stage RSAs, the RSA team should note adjacent land uses and their potential to generate substantial pedestrian volumes.

When assessing the width of a sidewalk, the RSA team should consider its usable width. Pedestrians rarely use the foot and a half of the sidewalk closest to the roadway or a building face. The RSA team should also pay attention to "choke points" that narrow the effective sidewalk width (e.g., street furniture, utility poles, poor transitions between developments, etc.).

A.1.5 Is there adequate separation between vehicular traffic and pedestrians?

Buffers can positively enhance both the perceived and actual safety of sidewalks by providing lateral separation between pedestrians and vehicular traffic. Since pedestrians typically prefer to be separated from traffic as much as possible, they may take alternate parallel paths when buffers are inadequate. Sometimes this results in pedestrians walking through landscaped areas where there is little danger to pedestrians. However, other times this results in pedestrians walking in parallel access roads and through parking areas.

Buffers can also improve accessibility by providing space for level sidewalk crossings across driveways. When landscaped, buffers may also deter pedestrians from crossing roads at unsafe locations. Wide buffers reduce pedestrian exposure to vehicle spray (as well as puddle splash) during wet weather, and also provide space for snow storage, both of which promote pedestrians' use of the sidewalk.

Often bridges are designed with only a curb separating pedestrians on the sidewalk from vehicular traffic. This measure alone is often inadequate as the curb does not form an adequate barrier between vehicular and pedestrian traffic. Vehicles traveling at speeds over 25 mph can mount a curb at relatively flat impact angles[12].

Although a narrower sidewalk might be adequate for many pedestrian uses, school children may require additional space since they often walk in groups. Insufficient sidewalk width can be a particular concern for younger children, who are easily distracted. In such situations, a wider sidewalk can greatly improve safety. This photo shows that a 5 foot wide sidewalk is barely sufficient for even a small group of school children, though the landscaped buffer strip provides additional separation from traffic.

The RSA team should consider the adequacy of the width of the buffer. Roadways with higher traffic speeds, several lanes, and greater traffic volumes should have wider buffers than narrow, low volume and low speed streets.

Parking lanes and bicycle lanes may help buffer pedestrians from vehicular traffic. The RSA team should consider potential unintended consequences resulting from all buffers, such as:

> ➤ **Large trees may be undesirable where lateral clearance to traffic is limited, or where traffic speeds are high.** In these cases they can form obstructions that limit sight distance to crossing pedestrians or to vehicles exiting driveways and intersecting streets, or can become fixed object hazards for motorists that depart from the travel lanes.

> ➤ **Pedestrians crossing midblock from on-street parking spaces can increase the risk of dart-out crashes.** This risk may be particularly high in areas where children are present.

Photos by: Dan Burden / www.pedpikeimages.org
The photo on the left shows a deep buffer with large trees that offers a safe and pleasant walking environment. The RSA team should check whether buffers such as this form sight distance obstructions to vehicles exiting driveways and intersecting streets. The photo on the right shows how curbside parking can effectively buffer the sidewalk from the travel lanes. The RSA team should check to see if traffic speeds may increase crash potential for this type of buffer.

A.1.6. Are sidewalk/street boundaries discernable to people with visual impairments?

Having a clearly defined walkway helps define pedestrian, bicycle and vehicle travel zones, and can reduce conflicts between vehicles and pedestrians with visual impairments. The RSA team should assess whether cues are present that indicate the boundary between the sidewalk and travel lane, such as detectable warnings that include color changes, tactile changes at crossings (see prompt B.1.10), and buffers. Discernable boundaries may be a particular issue on walkable shoulders, as there is no buffer between the travel way and shoulder and it may be difficult to provide tactile changes.

Photo by: ITE Pedestrian Bicycle Council
The picture on the left shows a sidewalk with a clear boundary between the sidewalk and street. The picture on the right shows a street where the sidewalk is made of the same material as the street, providing little contrast between the street and sidewalk, which may increase the potential of a conflict between pedestrians and vehicles.

A.1.7 Are ramps provided as an alternative to stairs?

Since stairs can be a problem for pedestrians with mobility impairments, the RSA team should evaluate whether alternatives, such as ramps, are provided and whether they are safe. Good designs include:

> Level landings at the top and bottom (and, for long ramps, at intermediate intervals) where people in wheelchairs can stop or turn around.

> Gradual, consistent slope.

> Free from cracks or breaks.

> Side rails where desirable or necessary.

RSA Examples

Buffers/pedestrian desire lines: *Pedestrians generally use the shortest or most convenient path (along "pedestrian desire lines"), or pathways that provide a comfortable separation from traffic.* Where pedestrian desire lines or other alternative pathways do not follow pedestrian facilities (such as sidewalks), pedestrians may cross roadways at potentially unsafe locations, or locations where drivers do not expect them.

Pictured above, a narrow sidewalk is provided adjacent to the roadway. A parallel worn path or "goat trail" where many pedestrians prefer to walk is clearly visible about 20 feet from the sidewalk. Pedestrians may choose to walk here instead of the sidewalk for a greater degree of separation from traffic, or convenience to other pedestrian attractors/generators. Future long term plans should consider formalizing a pedestrian path separated from the roadway.

RSA Examples (continued)

Sidewalk width: *Sidewalks should be wide enough to safely accommodate pedestrians of all ability types traveling in both directions.* Narrow sidewalks may be insufficient to accommodate two passing pedestrians, or to allow faster pedestrians to pass slower pedestrians. Where the sidewalk is narrow, some pedestrians may step into the roadway, where they may conflict with drivers or cyclists.

A pedestrian with a walker requires most of the sidewalk width provided. A pedestrian approaching from the opposite direction would have trouble passing on the sidewalk. Pedestrians were observed walking on the street and crossing mid block upstream of this pedestrian to provide her with sufficient walking room.

Absence of sidewalk: *Well-designed, accessible sidewalks should be provided on both sides of the street to minimize exposure of pedestrians to vehicular and bicycle traffic.* Where pedestrian facilities cannot be provided (either in the short term or long term), alternative facilities should be provided and pedestrians should be clearly directed to them.

A pedestrian is walking in the roadway on a high speed arterial. A sidewalk is missing from this side of the roadway because of lack of available right of way. Although a sidewalk is provided on the other side of the road, pedestrians were not observed to cross the street to reach the sidewalk because of the lack of a safe crossing. A short term suggestion could be to widen the median (where there is overhead lighting and sight distance) to provide an adequate refuge so pedestrians can cross one direction of traffic at a time to reach the sidewalk on the other side. A long term recommendation may be to revise lane and median widths so a sidewalk protected by a rigid barrier can be incorporated within the available cross section.

A.2 Quality, Conditions, and Obstructions

A.2.1 Will snow storage disrupt pedestrian access or visibility?

The RSA team should consider whether snow storage could block sidewalks or reduce pedestrian visibility. In particular, bus stops and curb cuts at street crossings should be clear of snow.

A.2.2. Is the path clear of both temporary and permanent obstructions?

Obstructions affect all pedestrians, but are particularly hazardous to pedestrians with mobility restrictions who may require additional space to navigate the sidewalk, or to pedestrians with limited vision who may fail to see the obstructions. The RSA team should consider whether obstructions prevent a wheelchair or other mobility aid (such as a walker, scooter, or stroller) from getting by.

There are two basic types of obstructions:

> **Movable and temporary (such as illegally parked cars, newspaper stands, delivery trucks, trash cans/dumpsters, portable signs, landscaping, or water/snow)**– Temporary obstructions may also include legal parking, such as a vehicle bumper overhanging the sidewalk, which may be addressed through design. These are typically addressed through maintenance, policy, and enforcement.

> **Fixed (such as utility poles, street furniture, street and commercial signs, objects projecting from buildings or phone booths)**–Fixed obstructions can be more difficult to move. These can be addressed through design and policy.

The RSA team should consider all types of obstructions and potential seasonal and event variations (in relation to temporary parking signs, etc.) when conducting an RSA.

RSA Examples

Surface obstructions: *Pedestrians, especially those with vision impairments or mobility restrictions, do not expect protruding objects on the sidewalk and may trip and fall as a result.* If a pedestrian with disabilities has knowledge that such a protrusion exists, they may elect to avoid such a route in favor of a seemingly safer route.

The sidewalk pictured may present a significant hazard to a pedestrian, because of (1) street furniture and equipment reducing the usable width of a sidewalk, and (2) an uneven sidewalk surface (with bricks, basement access doors and a manhole cover) that may be a challenge for mobility and sight impaired pedestrians. Consideration should be given for creating straight, uninterrupted paths free of obstacles that conform to pedestrian desire lines.

The sidewalk is partly obstructed by a fire hydrant (foreground) and utility pole (background). Although the sidewalk has been widened behind the hydrant, the usable sidewalk width may still be insufficient to accommodate a wheelchair. In addition to the minimum sidewalk clearance provided, the sidewalk is also near the maximum grade for wheelchair users. These compounding factors significantly increase the risk to pedestrians in wheelchairs. Further widening of the sidewalk can be considered.

A.2.3 Is the walking surface too steep?

Steep walking surfaces (both grades and cross slopes) can affect pedestrian stability and control, especially for persons with disabilities. Therefore, sidewalks should be designed to minimize slopes or provide intermittent level landings. The following two components of walking surface should be reviewed by the RSA team:

This combination of maximum cross slopes and roadway curvature can present a difficulty, especially for someone with limited visual abilities or in a wheelchair. The hazard is compounded by the fact that it provides access to a driveway.

> ➤ **Grade**—The slope of the walkway parallel to the roadway.

> ➤ **Cross slope**—The slope of a sidewalk perpendicular to the roadway often becomes a problem at driveways, especially for pedestrians in wheelchairs who must maintain a straight path.

A.2.4. Is the walking surface adequate and well-maintained?

Pedestrians may avoid or be unable to use poor walking surfaces. On existing facilities, the RSA team should determine if unsafe conditions exist, such as uneven surfaces, poor drainage, slippery surfaces, tripping hazards, or poor maintenance. More specifically, the RSA team should consider the following:

> **Surface smoothness**—Abrupt changes in level can create several problems for pedestrians, including tripping hazards. Even minor uplifts or lips in the pavement surface, can create challenges to accessibility for pedestrians using wheelchairs, canes, or pedestrians with limited visibility.

> **Drainage**—Sidewalks with poor drainage can create slippery surfaces that can be especially dangerous for the elderly and

Brick sidewalks can be susceptible to changes in level.

The photo on the left shows a depression in the sidewalk where there is an evaporated puddle. The picture on the right shows an existing puddle.

persons with disabilities. Drainage problems may be observed on existing facilities by the presence of puddles or, if the site visit is conducted in dry weather, accumulated sediment left from evaporated puddles.

> **Maintenance**—Poorly maintained sidewalks can cause injury to pedestrians. Cracked walkways with heavy tree roots, loose sand and debris, worn or slippery steps or ramp surfaces, and snow and ice all cause problems for pedestrians, and should be noted by the RSA team. Obstructions such as encroachment of overgrown trees or shrubs on walkways are seasonal and require regular maintenance.

Maintenance is important for maintaining accessibility of walking facilities.

A.3 Continuity and Connectivity

A.3.1 Are sidewalks/walkable shoulders continuous and on both sides of the street?

The RSA team should assess the continuity of the pedestrian network for a range of users. A discontinuous network can be impassable to wheelchairs, scooters, strollers, or to all users if it ends in an unpaved or unmaintained area that is wet, icy, muddy, or snowy. Where the pedestrian network is discontinuous, pedestrians may be diverted onto the roadway, where they may conflict with motorists and cyclists, or through paved parking areas where they may conflict with parking, entering, and departing vehicles. Discontinuities include the following:

> ➤ Missing sidewalks or gaps.
> ➤ Abrupt changes in sidewalk width.
> ➤ Obstructions on sidewalks (see prompt A.2).
> ➤ Frequent, abrupt changes in direction.

Sidewalks are sometimes provided only on one side of the street. When there is sidewalk only on one side of the street, pedestrians may cross the street at places where motorists are not expecting them or may walk in the street where they are more likely to conflict with vehicular traffic.

A.3.2. Are measures needed to direct pedestrians to safe crossing points and pedestrian access ways?

In areas with high-speed or high-volume traffic, there may be a need to channelize pedestrians to safe crossings to mitigate the potential of a severe pedestrian-vehicle crash. Pedestrians can be channeled by physical barriers, such as fencing, bollards, shrubs and other buffers, and/or by signs which direct them to appropriate crossings. Fencing should not pose a hazard to motorists (e.g., horizontal rails should not have the potential to spear a vehicle if struck) or bicyclists. The RSA team should also note whether shrubs and other plantings used to direct pedestrians could obstruct visibility or pose hazards to motorists.

RSA Examples

Gaps and discontinuities: *Transitions for pedestrian facilities are often neglected, especially at project limits and between developments.* Roadway transitions at project limits are usually carefully considered to ensure continuity and connectivity for motor vehicles. Less consideration may be given to pedestrian transitions (even on pedestrian-oriented projects) resulting in gaps, awkward elevation/alignment changes, or unnecessarily risky crossings that may occur in sidewalk and path networks. Alternatively, new pedestrian facilities may be introduced where no connecting facilities are provided at all, resulting in an abrupt sidewalk end.

The sidewalk in this photo ends abruptly just before the driveway, however a worn path or "goat trail" created by pedestrians can be seen continuing parallel to the roadway. Lack of connectivity such as this are impassable to wheelchairs, scooters, and strollers, and are especially susceptible to environmental changes, resulting in muddy paths or snowy conditions that divert pedestrians into the roadway or adjacent parking area, where they may conflict with motorists. The RSA team may suggest extending the sidewalk to close the gaps.

In this photo, a sidewalk is provided to access the bus stop in the foreground, but the sidewalk ends just beyond the driveway. The gap in the sidewalk network reduces pedestrian safety, comfort, and convenience. Pedestrians with disabilities or those who are pushing a stroller would be forced out onto the street, resulting in conflicts with motor vehicles. Extending the sidewalk could be suggested.

RSA Examples (continued)

Connectivity: *Transition areas from a walkable shoulder to a sidewalk are often inadequate. Transitions that are not clear may result in situations where pedestrians and drivers may not expect to share the roadway.*

Sidewalk connectivity: *Adequate, continuous sidewalks provide walking space for pedestrians and a clear, typically safer path.* Gaps in sidewalks may direct pedestrians into the roadway, where they may conflict with motorists and cyclists. Gaps may also make sidewalks impassible to pedestrians with disabilities.

A sidewalk ends at a driveway without providing an accessible connection to the walkable shoulder in the distance. Pedestrians, especially during and after rain storms, are forced to walk in the right turn lane as the landscaped area between facilities is sloped toward the open channel. The RSA team may provide suggestions for improving the safety of this connection.

The sidewalk in this photograph terminates in a right turn lane. Pedestrians must contend not only with right turning traffic, but traffic crossing their paths at the two access points located off of the lane. Motorists exiting these driveways are focused on finding a gap in traffic and avoiding conflicts with right turning vehicles and may not see pedestrians walking along the side of the road. The RSA team may suggest providing a continuous, level sidewalk through this area.

A.4 Lighting

A.4.1 Is the sidewalk adequately lit?

Street lighting can improve pedestrian visibility and create a sense of security. In urban areas, lighting should be provided continuously. In rural areas, it may only be necessary to provide lighting at pedestrian crossings such as intersections and mid-block crossings (see prompt B.4.1).

For RSAs of existing roads, the RSA team should conduct a nighttime site visit to assess the adequacy of pedestrian lighting. Obstacles such as trees may reduce the amount of light at street level or create interruptions in lighting, especially when light poles are taller than the trees. Adequate lighting is especially important on narrow pedestrian paths, underpasses and bridges where nighttime security is an issue.

A.4.2 Does street lighting improve pedestrian visibility at night?

In urban areas where pedestrians are more likely to cross mid-block (especially where on-street parking exists), lighting along the roadway is critical for helping motorists see pedestrians at marked and unmarked crossing points. The RSA team should evaluate the adequacy of the lighting along the roadway with respect to pedestrian volumes. The potential for jaywalking should be evaluated based on traffic generators, age of pedestrians, and social environment (e.g., are there drinking establishments/bars in the vicinity?).

A.5 Visibility

A.5.1 Is visibility of pedestrians walking on the sidewalk/shoulder adequate?

Visibility is a concern at crossings (see prompt B.5), driveways (see prompt A.6.1) and on walkable shoulders and sidewalks where there is no barrier between motorists, bicyclists, and pedestrians. Streets with on-street parking should also be checked for visibility of pedestrians on the sidewalk, since parked vehicles may not always be present.

A.6 Driveways

A.6.1 Are the conditions at driveways intersecting sidewalks endangering pedestrians?

Driveways often create multiple conflicts between pedestrians and motorists because drivers typically watch for other motor vehicles, not pedestrians. For instance, motorists seeking to make a right turn out of a parking lot may be looking for traffic approaching from the left and not look for pedestrians approaching from the right. Additionally, motorists that are backing out of a driveway may not be able to clearly see a pedestrian walking behind the car. There are several factors that increase the hazard potential for pedestrians at driveways; the most significant include:

A motorist backing out of the driveway would have a difficult time viewing pedestrians walking on the sidewalk.

> **Visibility**–In residential areas the RSA team should check for overgrown landscaping, fences, signs, and mailboxes around driveways, which may obstruct sightlines between pedestrians and drivers. Additionally, in commercial areas, the RSA team should assess whether buildings and dumpsters block driver and/or pedestrian sightlines. Visibility at driveways can also be reduced by parked vehicles (both legal and illegal).

> **Vehicle Speed**–High vehicle speeds increase the likelihood and severity of pedestrian-vehicle crashes at driveways. Vehicle speed is a function of driveway design.

Driveways with large corner radii may promote higher vehicle speeds into and out of the driveways, and increase the exposure of pedestrians to conflicting traffic by increasing the driveway crossing distance. The RSA team should review driveway radii with reference to the needs and safety of all road users (see prompt B.1.1).

Some commercial developments have no clearly defined driveways. More about potential issues related to access into developments can be found in Section C.

Driveways are a particular concern in areas with significant populations of younger pedestrians, such as around schools, playgrounds, parks and other areas frequented by children. When considering safety at driveways, the RSA team should take a 'child's eye' perspective and consider visibility at heights of 3 to 4 feet.

Cross slope issues at driveways are discussed in prompt A.2.3.

A.6.2 Does the number of driveways make the route undesirable for pedestrian travel?

Closely spaced driveways can deter pedestrians from walking on sidewalks. Instead, pedestrians may take unexpected paths which may put them into conflict with vehicular traffic in the roadway or on other routes. This is especially a problem in areas with high traffic volumes and high speeds, such as commercial areas. The RSA team should assess how the density of driveways affects pedestrian safety.

RSA Example

Pedestrian Visibility: Since drivers frequently do not expect pedestrians, they may fail to look for and accommodate them. Drivers typically watch for other motor vehicles at driveways and other access points, which are more visible because of their size and use of headlights. Drivers tend to be less observant of pedestrians, who are typically less visible and who can enter the roadway at unexpected locations and from unexpected directions.

A sidewalk crosses a driveway where entering and exiting drivers must watch for conflicting traffic and where drivers' sightlines are partly obstructed by parked vehicles, landscaping, and a railing (circled, far side of driveway). The steep grade and lack of visibility of traffic can draw a motorist's attention away from pedestrians walking along the sidewalk, creating a potentially high risk conflict. Removal of one of the factors that decrease visibility (e.g., railing or grade) would help improve safety. In this case replacing the railing with a more transparent design could be suggested.

A.7 Traffic Characteristics

A.7.1 Are there any conflicts between bicycles and pedestrians?

Conflicts between pedestrians and bicyclists may occur on streets, sidewalks, at crossings (see Section B), and at driveways (see prompt A.6.1). Bicycle/pedestrian collisions may result in substantial injury to both parties. Cyclists may be more likely to use sidewalks where roadway cycling is hazardous or unpleasant (such as where traffic volumes or speeds are high, or there is continuous on-street parking), or where the cyclists are young and inexperienced (such as around schools). The RSA team may look for elements that will contribute to the risk of bicycle/pedestrian conflicts, including high volumes of cyclists on the sidewalks, narrow sidewalks that cannot safely accommodate both modes of travel, locations where pedestrian facilities (sidewalks and crosswalks) intersect bicycle facilities such as bike paths and bike lanes, and mixed-use facilities where cyclists and pedestrians use adjoining sections of pavement.

A.8 Signs and Pavement Markings

Signs and pavement markings enhance the safety and comfort of the pedestrian environment. The standards for signing and pavement markings for pedestrians are described in the MUTCD. Knowledge of these standards is essential for the RSA team; however, the team is reminded that an RSA is not a standards check. The MUTCD does include a provision for state and local agencies to develop and install warning signs not specified in the MUTCD[13]. Common issues with signs and pavement markings along streets are described in this section. Signs and pavement markings related to crossings are described in Section B.

A.8.1 Are pedestrian travel zones clearly delineated from other modes of traffic through the use of striping, colored and/or textured pavement, signing, and other methods?

The RSA team should assess how clearly distinguished pedestrian travel zones are from other travel modes. Considerations for pedestrian travel zones are as follows:

> **Pedestrian facilities such as sidewalks.** Wayfinding signs are the most common sign used on sidewalks. These should clearly direct pedestrians on safe paths and crossings.

> **Special pedestrian routes such as footpaths and other shared-use facilities or roadways.** In rural areas, striping can be used to separate walkable shoulders from vehicular travel lanes. On shared-use paths, striping can be used to separate pedestrians from bicyclists.

> **Special pedestrian zones such as school zones.** Signage that is specific to school zones alerts drivers to the presence of school children. School zone signage includes lower speed limit signs for those times when school children are likely to be present, pavement markings, and yellow school 'pentagon' signs marking crosswalks.

The RSA team should also determine if posted signs still serve the intended purpose, i.e., they are not obsolete.

A.8.2 Is the visibility of signs and pavement markings adequate during the day and night?

Signs and pavement markings are only effective if they are readily visible to road users, especially at night when the visibility of pedestrians is diminished. Pedestrian sign visibility may be limited if signs are laterally positioned far from the travel lane, if they are placed after a horizontal or vertical curve, or if they are obstructed by other signs. Pedestrian pavement marking visibility (i.e., shoulder markings when no sidewalk is present) may be limited if markings are faded or worn, or do not provide a high degree of reflectivity. In RSAs of existing facilities, the RSA team may also identify poor sign visibility resulting from the following:

> Damage.

> Vandalism.

> Poor maintenance.

> Obstruction by vegetation or other structures.

Sign conspicuity may also be compromised if pedestrian signage must compete with adjacent commercial signage.

B. CROSSINGS

Overview

The prompts in this section are intended to help the RSA team identify pedestrian safety problems at crossings, which include both intersection and mid-block crossings.

Generally, prompts in this section will help the RSA team address the following:

> ➤ Is the visibility of pedestrians while in the crossing adequate?

> ➤ Does traffic control at crossings address the needs of all users?

> ➤ How do pedestrians interact with other modes of traffic at crossings?

This section of the guidebook provides a more detailed description of the specific prompts found in the prompt list for pedestrian safety at crossings. The section numbers correspond to the numbered prompt lists.

Terminology used in this section include:

Formal pedestrian crossings

Intersections, both signalized and unsignalized- intersection crossings are almost always considered formal, legal crossings because there is an implied crosswalk for pedestrians at every intersection, whether or not the crosswalk is marked.

Midblock- Formal midblock crossings are marked with a crosswalk and may have additional features that identify them as crossings, such as signs, curb extensions, and curb ramps.

Informal pedestrian crossings

Locations where it is obvious that pedestrians are crossing regularly but where markings and possibly curb ramps are absent.

B.1 Presence, Design, and Placement

B.1.1 Do wide curb radii lengthen pedestrian crossing distances and encourage high-speed right turns?

The RSA team should evaluate whether curb radii are appropriate for given/anticipated pedestrian volumes and traffic mix. Wider radii may reduce the safety of the pedestrian environment by:

> ➤ Encouraging high-speed right turns.
> ➤ Increasing the crossing distance for pedestrians.
> ➤ Reducing the pedestrian waiting area.
> ➤ Creating an environment where pedestrians and motorists find it difficult to see each other.

This illustration shows the effect of curb radius on crossing distance. Smaller curb radii shorten the crossing distance and provide a tighter turn.

> ➤ Reducing visibility of stop signs due to greater offset from travel lanes.
> ➤ Failing to effectively direct traffic due to the wide paved area.

Curb radii balance the requirements of pedestrian safety with the needs of large vehicles and emergency service vehicles, which may require wide curb radii to turn. Curb radii should accommodate vehicles that commonly use the intersection, as well as emergency vehicles. The RSA team may wish to consult local emergency services, especially if an emergency response facility is in or close to the study area or the RSA team is aware that curb radii may be an issue.

B.1.2 Do channelized right turn lanes minimize conflicts with pedestrians?

Channelized right turn lanes can enhance pedestrian safety by allowing pedestrians to cross the right-turn lane separately, using the channelizing island for refuge. However, significant pedestrian safety issues may arise if the channelized right turn lane is designed to favor the movement of vehicular traffic by including geometric features that facilitate high-speed turns by right-turning traffic, such as:

> ➤ A wide turn radius.
> ➤ Flat entry angle entering and/or leaving the right turn.
> ➤ Exclusive receiving lane.
> ➤ Wide lanes.

The RSA team should check for the following issues when evaluating the safety of a channelized right turn lane:

Some channelized right turns act as free-flow right turn lanes, potentially creating pedestrian-vehicle conflicts. The crossing pedestrian in the photograph must walk between vehicles in the right-turn traffic flow.

> ➤ **High Traffic Volumes**–Often, channelized right turn lanes are created to increase the right turn capacity at an intersection. As a result, turn volumes may be high giving pedestrians little opportunity to safely cross.
> ➤ **Traffic Speeds**–The geometry may promote higher vehicle speeds, which makes it difficult for pedestrians to judge gaps in traffic and increases the potential for a severe crash.
> ➤ **Driver Attention Focused to the Left Side, not Front, of Vehicle**–Drivers turning from a channelized right-turn lane typically look leftward for gaps in through traffic, and may fail to observe pedestrians approaching or entering the crosswalk from their right.

B.1.3 Does a skewed intersection direct drivers' focus away from crossing pedestrians?

Intersecting roads meeting at an angle other than 90 degrees are called skewed intersections. The greater the intersection skew, the more drivers must turn their heads to observe crossing traffic. Drivers looking far to one side may fail to observe pedestrians in the crosswalk, or entering the crosswalk from the other side of the street. The risk of collision may be increased where driver and pedestrian movements are not controlled by a traffic signal and where vehicles are permitted to turn right on red.

B.1.4 Are pedestrian crossings located in areas where sight distance may be a problem?

Sufficient stopping sight distance should be available on the approaches to all pedestrian crossings. Even where stopping sight distance meets the minimum AASHTO policy values, a greater sight distance may be desirable to improve pedestrian safety where:

> ➤ Pedestrian visibility is limited by poor lighting.
> ➤ A substantial number of child pedestrians are expected.
> ➤ Pedestrian crossings are infrequent and therefore unexpected by drivers.

Areas of particular concern include crest vertical curves and horizontal curves, where sight distance is often limited.

The RSA team should consider the location of crossings with respect to the geometric alignment, especially in areas where minimum geometric standards may not be consistently met or maintained, and in rural areas where pedestrians are less common.

RSA Examples

Curb radii / crosswalk markings: *Pedestrians waiting to cross streets should be afforded waiting areas outside of the travel paths of vehicles.* Wide curb radii may result in a wide expanse of pavement where pedestrian and vehicle pathways are not clear. Poorly placed crosswalk markings can exacerbate this problem, creating a false sense of security for pedestrians.

The street and crosswalk design at the stop controlled intersection in this photo creates potential conflicts between vehicles and motorists by encouraging pedestrians to wait in the street when crossing both legs of the intersection as shown. The RSA team may suggest placing a channelized island with pedestrian refuge or reducing the curb radius to reduce crossing distance and slow down right turn traffic.

RSA Examples (continued)

Curb radii/crossing distance: *Curb radii should adequately consider all users.* Curb radii should be designed to consider expected traffic mix, volumes, and types. Curb radii should accommodate common vehicle types turning right without mounting the corner curb, not the exceptional vehicle. Consideration should be given to expected pedestrian volumes and abilities of pedestrians. The smaller curb radii reduce pedestrian crossing distances and slow vehicles turning right.

The curb radii at the intersection in this photo are small, minimizing the crosswalk length and reducing pedestrian exposure to vehicular traffic. This residential street, with young and elderly pedestrians, is a good location for short curb radii. Access for emergency vehicles has been maintained by utilizing a low curb profile on the corners with pavers, which allows emergency vehicles to mount the curb.

Location of pedestrian crossings: *Crosswalks and other designated pedestrian crossings should be located so that they are readily visible to approaching drivers.* The RSA team should review crossing locations with reference to their visibility under all weather and lighting conditions, and at all seasons. Crossing points that are readily apparent during the day may be less apparent at night. Seasonal factors (such as summer foliage or winter snowbanks) may also compromise visibility. The RSA team should also consider visibility at "unofficial" crossings that reflect pedestrian desire lines, but are not necessarily marked or otherwise designated.

The crossing is positioned beyond a horizontal curve. Drivers such as the one in the photo are unlikely to see the crossing (which is not marked by signs or pavement markings) until they are exiting the curve, at which point drivers are typically accelerating. The curve also limits the distance at which headlights would illuminate the crossing, so the risk of a pedestrian crash is increased at night. Also, a pedestrian crossing toward the camera is facing away from vehicles approaching around the curve, and may consequently be less aware of them. Finally, the curb ramps are offset, increasing exposure of pedestrians and increasing the difficulty of the crossing for someone with visual limitations. The RSA team may suggest moving this crossing away from the curve and place the curb ramps directly across from each other.

A well marked crosswalk (far side) ends at a sidewalk that is partly obstructed by a signal pole and terminates at a barrier curb with no ramp. Wheelchair users have to share the road with vehicles to get around the island and are not able to reach the push button (circled). Even pedestrians without visible mobility restrictions avoided this island.

B.1.5 Do raised medians provide a safe waiting area (refuge) for pedestrians ?

Raised medians or crossing islands are areas that separate lanes of traffic. They provide a safe waiting place for pedestrians, reduce the crossing distance and separate the crossing into two or more phases. This helps reduce the complexity of the crossing and pedestrian exposure to traffic, especially at midblock crossings, where motorists may not expect pedestrians.

If a raised median or island is present, the RSA team should assess whether the median refuge is:

> Accessible to all pedestrians (e.g., has curb ramps or cut throughs and appropriate widths for wheelchair users).

> Large enough to accommodate peak pedestrian volumes.

> Large enough to accommodate a waiting or turning wheelchair on a level area.

> Utilized by pedestrians.

The raised median above is accessible to all pedestrians and provides a large waiting area.

At signalized intersections where pedestrian signals must be activated by a push button, an accessible push button should be placed on the median to accommodate pedestrians waiting there.

B.1.6 Are supervised crossings adequately staffed by qualified crossing guards?

Supervised crossings can be an effective means of increasing pedestrian safety, especially in school zones. If a crossing is supervised, the RSA team should evaluate the following:

> Are crossing guards wearing appropriate attire or carrying appropriate devices to be readily visible (including at dawn or dusk, if the crossing is supervised during low-light conditions)?

> Are crossing guards following established procedures?

> Are crossing guards able to communicate effectively with motorists and pedestrians?

> Do crossing guards command the respect of both pedestrians and motorists?

> Is the crossing supervised during the critical period for pedestrian traffic?

> Is the crossing supervised during the peak period of vehicular traffic?

> Are vulnerable users considered? The RSA team should evaluate the intersection during both supervised and unsupervised periods to identify all issues.

Stop signs and vests are important cues to inform drivers about a supervised pedestrian crossing.

B.1.7 Are marked crosswalks wide enough?

At marked crossings, especially signalized intersections where pedestrians queue until released, pedestrians often walk in groups and in opposite directions. The RSA team should evaluate whether crosswalk widths are sufficient so that pedestrians do not have to walk outside of crosswalk. In areas with many pedestrian destinations the crosswalks may need to be wider. Insufficient crosswalk widths can be a greater problem in locations with heavy traffic congestion or a significant number of turning movement conflicts, or in intersections of complex design.

B.1.8 Do at-grade railroad crossings accommodate pedestrians safely?

Pedestrian-train crashes are nearly always fatal, so the potential for such crashes should be investigated by the RSA team. In areas where pedestrians must cross a railroad track, the RSA team should consider the following:

- At controlled crossings, do barriers, gates, lights, and/or bells activate in time for all pedestrians (including pedestrians with disabilities) to clear the tracks? At uncontrolled crossings, is sufficient sight distance available to allow pedestrians to clear the tracks before an approaching train? Clearance time may depend in part on train speeds and the width of the crossing (especially where multiple tracks are present).
- At controlled crossings, can pedestrians exit the track area after barriers or gates have been lowered?
- Are deaf or hearing-impaired pedestrians safely accommodated?
- Is the pedestrian path across the tracks clear for sight-impaired pedestrians? Can pedestrians with low vision reasonably be expected to safely negotiate the uneven walking surface?
- Are the track surroundings slippery when wet, due to the materials used or to the presence of oil products?
- Do informal footpaths cross the railroad tracks at uncontrolled locations?
- Is there fencing/signage that restricts pedestrians from certain areas and are any pedestrians not obeying these restrictions?
- Do gates prevent pedestrians from crossing the tracks (from both sides of the street)?
- Where tracks cross the pedestrian pathway at an angle, can wheelchair users align their wheels at a right angle to the tracks when crossing, so that wheels are not caught in the space between the pavement and tracks?

The photo at left shows a railroad crossing with lights and gates extending across the nearside travel lanes and sidewalk. For a pedestrian approaching the crossing from the far side of the track (i.e., walking toward the camera, on the same side of the road as the photographer), the gate in the photograph is positioned beyond the railroad crossing, and only the back of the signal is visible. Consequently, a pedestrian (especially one with a visual impairment) may unintentionally walk into or wait within the track area when the crossing is activated. The photo on the right shows tactile warnings that help pedestrians with impairments identify the crossing.

B.1.9 Are crosswalks sited along pedestrian desire lines?

The RSA team should determine whether painted crosswalks are located along pedestrian desire lines. Painted crosswalks aligned with pedestrian desire lines encourage pedestrians to cross within the crosswalk, where drivers are more likely to expect them, and help pedestrians with vision impairments to more easily cross within the marked crosswalk. Poorly located crosswalks, such as that shown at right, may increase the risk of a pedestrian collision where vehicles are permitted to turn right on red.

B.1.10 Are corners and curb ramps appropriately planned and designed at each approach to the crossing?

Pedestrians may fail to use marked crosswalk that are not aligned with pedestrian desire lines. In this example, the pedestrian is following the alignment of the sidewalks, avoiding the inconveniently located crosswalk. In addition to being inconvenient, the location of this marked crosswalk may increase the collision risk for pedestrians using it. The crosswalk is set back from the intersection, and is consequently well outside the cone of vision for drivers turning right or left at the intersection. Drivers waiting in the intersection to turn may not observe the crosswalk set back, and therefore may fail to anticipate pedestrians crossing.

Curb ramps are sloped sections at curbs that provide a smooth transition from the sidewalk height to street level. They increase the safety and accessibility of sidewalk and crossing facilities for children, pedestrians with disabilities, and those with strollers. The RSA team should ask the following questions:

➤ Are curb ramps provided for each crossing?

➤ Are curb ramps located within the crosswalk markings, so that pedestrians using the ramp do not need to go outside the markings when entering or exiting the crosswalk?

> ➤ Are ramps aligned with the crosswalk, so that pedestrians (especially those with low vision) are correctly oriented when entering the crosswalk from the ramp?

> ➤ Is a level area of sufficient size provided at the top of the ramp to allow wheelchair users (or persons using wheeled dollies) to wait or maneuver without the risk of rolling into the roadway?

Curb ramps and cut throughs are oriented directly in line with the crosswalks, so that pedestrians do not need to walk outside the crosswalk markings when entering or leaving the crosswalk. The ramps correctly orient pedestrians with low vision along the crosswalk alignment when they are entering the crosswalk.

RSA Example

Peak pedestrian traffic: Pedestrian facilities should accommodate regular pedestrian peaks. The RSA team should be aware of land uses in the area that could regularly generate transient peaks in pedestrian volumes, such as schools, theaters, bus and transit stations, or workplaces that employ a shift-based workforce. At signalized intersections, sidewalks and crosswalks must accommodate waiting pedestrians who accumulate during the pedestrian "Don't Walk" phase and cross as a large group. Sidewalks and crosswalks may need to accommodate dismounted cyclists with bicycles, which require substantially more space than a pedestrian.

The narrow crosswalk likely meets minimum requirements for crosswalk width, but cannot accommodate three pedestrians walking abreast. The crosswalk markings should align with the ramp at the far side of the intersection, so that pedestrians entering the roadway from the ramp are within the crosswalk markings. The RSA team may suggest applying high visibility crosswalk markings of sufficient width to accommodate pedestrian volumes.

B.2 Quality, Condition, and Obstructions

The issues described in prompt A.2 apply to obstruction and protruding object considerations at crossings.

B.2.1 Is the crossing pavement adequate and well maintained?

The RSA team should consider whether walking surfaces are adequate and well-maintained, such as:

> - Are crossings free from poor drainage/puddles, slippery surfaces, and cracks or other discontinuities in the pavement that could trip pedestrians or snag wheelchairs?

> - Is non-slip material used for the pavement marking associated with the pedestrian facilities?

> - Does the crown in the road adversely affect pedestrians with mobility impairments who are crossing the road?

> - Do steep grades, either perpendicular or parallel to crossings, cause problems for pedestrians, especially those in wheelchairs?

B.2.2 Is the crossing pavement flush with the roadway surface?

The RSA team should verify that curb ramps are flush with street surfaces and that gaps and discontinuities are avoided at each crossing. Material changes between the street and the curb may leave a gap or crack that may be a tripping hazard, or obstruct a wheelchair, stroller, or dolly. Gaps or cracks can be especially critical at an unsignalized crossing where pedestrians have difficulty finding gaps in traffic, since efforts to get over or around a gap may increase the crossing time, increasing the pedestrian's exposure to conflicting traffic.

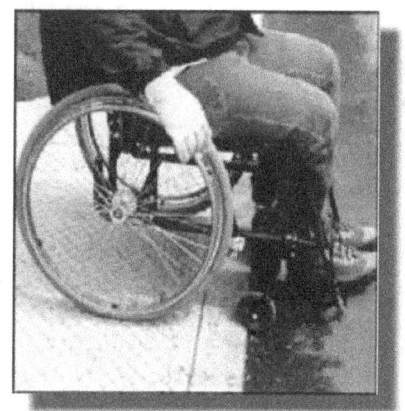

Photo by Michael Ronkin
Surfaces that are not flush can present an obstacle to a person in a wheelchair and also a tripping hazard to other pedestrians.

RSA Examples

Sidewalk-street transitions/year-round accessibility: *Pedestrian facilities should be usable under all weather conditions.* Most pedestrian facilities must accommodate pedestrians continually. Consequently, they should be able to accommodate users in all seasons and under all weather conditions. Sidewalks, crosswalks, median breaks and refuges, and grade-separated facilities should be reviewed to determine whether they are usable year-round, and in rain or snow.

Poor drainage results in an accumulation of water at the foot of the pedestrian ramp. Pedestrians attempting to avoid the water may enter or leave the crosswalk outside the markings. In cold weather, the water may form ice, generating a risk of slipping for pedestrians as they enter or leave the roadway. Pedestrians using this ramp will not be properly aligned with either crosswalk (a potential risk for blind pedestrians who cannot see the crosswalk alignment).

Maintenance issues: *Pedestrian facilities should be well maintained to keep travel surfaces smooth and clear. Pedestrian facilities that have been poorly maintained may be difficult or impossible to use, particularly for pedestrians with mobility, visual, and hearing impairments.* Pedestrian facilities that should be reviewed for adequate maintenance include sidewalks, curb ramps, pedestrian signal heads and push buttons, median refuges and breaks, grade-separated pedestrian crossings (including access to them), and driveway crossings. Maintenance issues are particularly common at road and driveway intersections, where pedestrian facilities such as sidewalks and push buttons are subject to strikes or loading by turning vehicles.

These curb ramps are cracked and rough, probably from loading by vehicles turning right at the intersection. The cracked surface presents a tripping hazard for all pedestrians, and may make it more difficult for pedestrians in wheelchairs to maneuver on the sloped sidewalk.

B.3 Continuity and Connectivity

B.3.1 Does pedestrian network connectivity continue through crossings by means of adequate waiting areas at corners, curb ramps and marked crosswalks?

Safe pedestrian networks include well-connected and continuous pedestrian facilities at crossings. Discontinuities at crossings may cause pedestrians to cross away from the desired crossing point and put them into conflict with vehicles and bicyclists. When evaluating crossings, the RSA team should determine the following:

- ➤ Is the waiting area sufficient to accommodate pedestrians, including those in wheelchairs or using strollers, during peak pedestrian times?

- ➤ Are ramps provided in accessible locations on the sidewalk?

- ➤ Do ramps direct pedestrians into the crosswalk, if present?

- ➤ Are pedestrians allowed to cross all legs of an intersection? If pedestrians are not allowed to cross a leg because of safety reasons, are they clearly directed to a convenient alternative crossing location?

- ➤ Are there marked crosswalks? See prompt B.1.7 and B.8 for more details on marked crosswalks.

Photo by Mike Cynecki
The photo above shows a good example of a sidewalk with an appropriate waiting area for pedestrians and an adequate curb ramp. A stand-back line has been painted to direct pedestrians where to wait to reduce the risk of conflicts with right-turning vehicles (including school buses, which require a larger turning radius) and passing pedestrians.

B.3.2 Are pedestrians clearly directed to crossing points and pedestrian access ways?

Pedestrian crossings should be clear and direct. Large suburban areas may require signing and channelizing fencing to direct pedestrians to safe crossings and obstruct unsafe crossings. Fencing and other directional treatments must not pose a hazard to motorists.

RSA Examples

Pedestrian network continuity: *The components of a pedestrian network should allow pedestrians to follow direct and continuous paths without unnecessary and unsafe diversions.*

A sidewalk ends in the right through lane on the exit leg of an intersection. Pedestrians wanting to cross the intersection to their left (to the right in the photograph) must walk in the roadway on the exit leg before crossing the channelized right turn lane, where no crosswalk has been provided.

Accessibility: *Pedestrian facilities may not be accessible to all users.* Persons with disabilities, and elderly or very young pedestrians, may have special needs. The RSA team should assess pedestrian facilities with regard to the needs of all road users.

A visual warning has been provided at this curb ramp to facilitate crossings by visually impaired pedestrians. However, the grate, which represents a hazard or obstacle to these pedestrians, has not been relocated. The grate can catch the tip of a cane or wheelchair casters. The RSA team may suggest placing two ramps on this corner, each directed across one leg of the intersection. The grate may be able to remain in between the two ramps.

As seen in the photograph, the accessible ramp is not aligned with the crosswalk and newspaper stands obstruct the section of the sidewalk in the path of the crosswalk, forcing pedestrians to walk outside of the crosswalk. This problem is exacerbated by the number of vehicles observed stopping beyond the stop bar and in or near the crosswalk.

B.4 Lighting

B.4.1 Is the pedestrian crossing adequately lit?

Visibility of pedestrians is typically at its lowest at night. Many pedestrians, especially children, are unaware of their own limited visibility. Adequate lighting can improve pedestrian visibility during the nighttime, and can improve the visibility of other road users (including cyclists) for pedestrians. The RSA team should assess lighting conditions at night to determine whether lighting allows drivers, cyclists, and pedestrians to readily see one another on the approaches to, and in, pedestrian crossings. When assessing lighting, potential issues an RSA team should consider are as follows:

> ➤ Is overhead lighting activated by a photocell or an automatic timer? Lights activated by photocells are responsive to ambient light levels, and may consequently be more reliable at dawn and dusk.

> ➤ Is lighting adequate during both peak and non-peak traffic conditions (applies especially during winter months)?

> ➤ Could lighting from adjacent commercial premises distract drivers, create glare, or compete with overhead lighting to reduce the effectiveness of the roadway lighting?

> ➤ Is "smart lighting" in proper working order (e.g., are pedestrians detected automatically and is response fast enough to capture pedestrian crossing)?

Smart lighting is lighting that increases intensity when a pedestrian uses a crossing equipped with this technology. Smart lighting may be pushbutton activated or can be employed using automatic pedestrian detection devices.

B.5 Visibility

B.5.1 Can pedestrians see approaching vehicles at all legs of the intersection/crossing and vice versa?

The RSA team must consider visibility from the perspective of all roadway users at crossings, especially children and persons in wheelchairs, who may be lower to the ground. Sight lines between all users must be free from obstructions. Visibility can be obstructed by a multitude of features that can be man made, natural, temporary, or permanent. The RSA team should consider the following:

> ➤ Do permanent fixed objects reduce visibility of pedestrians? These include:
>> ▹ Buildings.
>> ▹ Fences and barriers.
>> ▹ Signs and utility poles.
>> ▹ Bus shelters.

> ➤ Could temporary objects reduce visibility of pedestrians? These include:
>> ▹ Legally and illegally parked or loading vehicles.
>> ▹ Retail displays.
>> ▹ Dumpsters or other garbage receptacles.
>> ▹ Newspaper boxes.

> ➤ Could seasonal changes create conditions that may reduce visibility of pedestrians? These include:
>> ▹ Snow storage.
>> ▹ Seasonal changes in landscaping.

The risk associated with obstructed sightlines may be aggravated by a high driver workload, driver distraction (especially for drivers turning left or right), or failure to expect pedestrians.

B.5.2 Is the distance from the stop (or yield) line to a crosswalk sufficient for drivers to see pedestrians?

Stop or yield lines positioned too close to a crosswalk may result in limited pedestrian visibility as follows:

➤ **Vehicles in adjacent lanes may obstruct drivers' view of pedestrians in the crosswalk.** Stop or yield lines should be placed far enough from a crosswalk to allow an approaching driver to see a pedestrian crossing even when a vehicle is stopped in an adjacent lane.

➤ **Truck drivers stopped close to the crosswalk may fail to see pedestrians in the crosswalk in front of their vehicle, due to the height of the cab.** Stop or yield lines should be placed far enough from the crosswalk to allow truck drivers to see pedestrians, especially children or people in wheelchairs, passing or stopped in front.

B.5.3 Do other conditions exist where stopped vehicles may obstruct visibility of pedestrians?

Similar to the conditions described in prompt B.5.2, other typically less common conditions may arise where stopped vehicles may obstruct visibility of pedestrians. For example, on roads with wide lanes or shoulders a vehicle stopping for a pedestrian may be passed without the driver in the passing vehicle realizing a pedestrian is in the roadway. This is especially hazardous at unsignalized intersections, where the following driver may think that the front vehicle has stopped to wait for a gap to make a left turn.

RSA Examples

Pedestrian visibility–intersections: *Objects at the side of the road or in the median may obstruct sightlines between approaching drivers and pedestrians entering the roadway. Objects may include trees and other landscaping, street furniture such as signal cabinets and transit shelters, utility poles, signs, buildings, and snow banks. The risk associated with obstructed sightlines may be aggravated by driver distraction. Objects may also be transient or temporary, such as parked vehicles and stopped buses.*

In the intersection shown above, a tree partially obstructs the view of pedestrians waiting to cross the street. Motorists approaching this intersection to turn right focus their attention on finding a gap in traffic by looking for approaching conflicting vehicles to their left.

Pedestrian visibility—midblock crossings: *Pedestrians are not always clearly visible or expected by motorists at midblock pedestrian crossing locations. A number of transient conditions or events could obscure the visibility of pedestrians to vehicular traffic. Lighting, seasonal growth of vegetation, traffic congestion, and stopped vehicles or buses are just a few conditions that can temporarily increase the risk to pedestrians crossing a street by creating a sight obstruction. The risk associated with obstructed sightlines may be aggravated by driver expectance or distraction. Safety at pedestrian crossings must consider all permanent and transient conditions that may exist.*

The line of sight between vehicles and pedestrians standing at this midblock crosswalk (picture taken standing at the end of the ramp leading to the crosswalk) is blocked by the bus at the bus stop. When there are no buses present at the stop, there do not appear to be obstructed sight lines. The RSA team may suggest moving the bus stop to the far side of the crossing.

Pedestrian visibility–stopped vehicles: *Multiple lane facilities and two-way streets where same direction passing occurs can create a situation where a stopped vehicle obstructs the view of crossing pedestrians to a same direction passing vehicle.*

Motorists rarely yield to pedestrians waiting to cross this unmarked crossing. When a motorist does yield to pedestrians at the crossing, following drivers sometimes pass the stopped vehicle, increasing the risk of a multiple threat pedestrian collision. The width of the lane (over 15 feet) may encourage drivers to pass since they will not conflict with oncoming traffic. Due to traffic speeds, the RSA team may suggest placing a crosswalk, pedestrian warning signs, other pavement markings, and advance yield lines as a short term measure, and a signalized crossing as a long term measure.

RSA Examples (continued)

Pedestrian visibility/other obstructions: *Pedestrian visiblity can be compromised by other factors such as guardrails and buildings.*

Buildings sometimes extend to the edge of or beyond the property line, obstructing sight lines around corners. Drivers and crossing pedestrians may have a very limited view of one another. Motorists and pedestrians should have clear, unobstructed sight lines along the entire crosswalk. Vehicles turning right from this high speed arterial may not be able to stop in time to avoid a crash with a pedestrian in the crosswalk. The RSA team may suggest installing a bulb out and moving the crosswalk to where the building will not obstruct visibility of pedestrians in the crosswalk.

Guardrail, especially when combined with vertical and horizontal curvature, can obstruct visibility of pedestrians, particularly children and those in wheelchairs. This pedestrian waiting to cross can just barely see approaching vehicles (circled) over the guardrail from his location. The fact that the pedestrian is trying to cross a free flow right turn lane increases the risk of collision.

B.6 Access Management

B.6.1 Are driveways placed close to crossings?

Driveways may create multiple conflicts between pedestrians and motorists because entering and exiting drivers typically watch for other motor vehicles, not pedestrians. Driveways that are in close proximity to street crossings create multiple conflict points within a small area and can cause confusion between pedestrians and motorists. The RSA team should look for the following conditions that may occur when driveways are placed close to crossings:

Crossings at Intersections

Motorists cutting through corner properties with driveways on two legs may generate higher driveway volumes and speeds than expected, increasing the potential for a crash.

Midblock Crossings

Driveways placed between the stop bar and pedestrian crossing at mid-block crossings can be especially hazardous to pedestrians. Vehicles waiting to turn right from a driveway in such a location may be focusing their attention to the left to look for gaps in approaching traffic. When the approaching traffic has to stop for a red signal, the motorist could quickly turn into the path of pedestrians using the crossing.

B.7 Traffic Characteristics

B.7.1 Do turning vehicles pose a hazard to pedestrians?

Motorists leaving the access near this signalized midblock crossing may not expect pedestrians to be in front of them after executing the right turn.

Turning movements at intersections can be one of the most significant hazards to pedestrians. Potential hazards the RSA team should look for are as follows:

> Are turning vehicles yielding to pedestrians?

> Is sufficient timing provided to allow pedestrians and turning vehicles to clear the intersection?

The RSA team should to consider how signal phasing, timing, and turn movements affect pedestrian safety.

B.7.2 Are there sufficient gaps in the traffic to allow pedestrians to cross the road?

Traffic volumes, signal timings, and the presence of high-volume driveways determine whether there are sufficient gaps in the traffic to allow pedestrians to safely cross the street at midblock locations. Raised medians and islands can allow pedestrians to cross the road halfway when gaps in traffic exist in one direction (see prompt B.2.2). The RSA team should assess whether there are sufficient gaps in traffic for pedestrians to safely cross at unsignalized intersections and midblock locations.

Left-turning and right-turning traffic often conflicts with pedestrians crossing at signalized intersections. These conflicts can be the most significant hazard to a pedestrian crossing the intersection.

B.7.3 Do traffic operations (especially during peak periods) create a safety concern for pedestrians?

Traffic conditions such as limited gaps, high turning volumes, long queues, and high speeds may create safety issues for pedestrians. Traffic operations should be considered at various times of the day (such as commuter peaks), days of week (for example, near a shopping center), and seasons (for example, in a resort community). Operational issues affecting safety may vary at different times at a single location. For example, high turning volumes and long queues at an intersection may affect pedestrian safety during commuter peaks, whereas high speeds may affect pedestrian safety during off-peak times at the same intersection.

Conditions may be observed in the field (RSAs of existing facilities), or estimated by referring to anticipated volumes or traffic simulations (design-stage RSAs).

RSA Examples

Traffic congestion (right): Traffic congestion can often be so severe that vehicles are trapped on crosswalks. Traffic may not only block crosswalks at signalized intersections, but also may block unsignalized intersection crossings and midblock crossings.

Impact of traffic operations on pedestrians (bottom): Traffic operations may affect pedestrian safety. Even in the presence of well-designed and well-maintained pedestrian facilities, the operational characteristics of traffic may compromise pedestrian safety. Typical operational issues include high traffic speeds, and long queues or high turning volumes that interfere with pedestrian movements. These operational impacts may be specific to peak or off-peak periods.

A traffic queue extends through the intersection, obstructing the crosswalk during the pedestrian WALK interval. Pedestrians in or entering the crosswalk may conflict with drivers attempting to clear the intersection as the queue clears. In addition, the queued vehicles obstruct sightlines between pedestrians crossing the intersection and passing vehicular traffic.

The two photos show a vehicle making a permissive left turn in front of oncoming traffic and nearly hitting pedestrians in a crosswalk during the WALK interval. The RSA team may suggest providing a protected left turn that does not conflict with the pedestrian WALK interval.

B.8 Signs and Pavement Markings

Signs and pavement markings may enhance the safety and comfort of the pedestrian environment[14]. The standards for signing and pavement markings for pedestrians are described in the MUTCD and state supplements. While knowledge of these standards is critical for the RSA team, the team is reminded that an RSA is not a simple standards check. Common issues with signs and pavement markings are described in this section.

B.8.1 Is paint on stop bars and crosswalks worn, or are signs worn, missing, or damaged?

Signs and pavement markings are important elements of pedestrian safety, since they advise drivers of the presence of pedestrians on the road, and delineate pedestrian pathways in and close to the roadway, such as walkable shoulders and crosswalks. Worn pavement markings and faded, damaged, or missing signs may fail to serve their intended purpose when drivers cannot see them. Worn signs and pavement markings may be particularly difficult for drivers to see at night (if the retroreflectivity of the sign is limited) or in wet weather (when a film of water can reduce the visibility and reflectivity of pavement markings). The RSA team should endeavor to observe signs and pavement markings under these conditions to assess their visibility.

B.8.2 Are crossing points for pedestrians properly signed and/or marked?

The RSA team should determine whether pavement marking and signing is appropriate at crossings (consult also prompt B.9.1 for signalized crossings). Signing and pavement markings should consider vehicle speeds, volume of pedestrians and vehicular traffic volumes. The RSA team should also determine if there are signs or pavement markings that are confusing to motorists or pedestrians, or

A pedestrian crossing at an intersection can be either marked (e.g., designated by paint) or unmarked. An unmarked crossing is defined as the extension of the sidewalks at the intersection.

that are not obeyed. For example, "No Pedestrian Crossing" (R9-3) signs, and signs directing pedestrians where to cross, may not prevent pedestrians from crossing at unsafe locations. Other examples of what the RSA team should look for are described as follows:

Signs

> Regulatory signs, such as "Yield Here to Pedestrians," inform motorists and pedestrians of their legal responsibilities on the road. However, signs alone are typically insufficient to address safety issues. The RSA team should determine if regulatory signs have been used to attempt to solve a safety problem on an RSA of an existing facility.

> Warning signs, such as "School Bus Stop Ahead" or Pedestrian Warning Signs, are intended to advise motorists of the presence of pedestrians. Overuse of signs, or signs that are no longer relevant, diminish the effectiveness of all similar signs, even in other locations.

> Guide signs and street signs provide directional and location information to both motorists and pedestrians, and should be visible to pedestrians as well as motorists.

Regulatory signs may also be illuminated signs which operate only under specific conditions or specific times of the day.

Pavement Markings

The RSA team should determine whether pavement marking (both crosswalk markings and pavement word markings) are clearly visible to pedestrians to help direct pedestrians to intended crossings. Marked crosswalks should also be direct to minimize pedestrian exposure to traffic.

The RSA team should also look at pavement markings from a driver's perspective. Standard pavement markings may fade quickly, and are often not noticed or understood by motorists. Textured pavement crosswalk markings can also be less visible to motorists and can easily be mistaken for an area that has been repaired.

The photo on the left shows a textured pavement crosswalk (detail on the right) that is similar in color to the adjacent road pavement. The textured pavement is visible to pedestrians, but drivers may mistake the crosswalk treatment for a utility cut or other pavement patch.

RSA Example

Crosswalk markings: *Marked crosswalks should be placed along pedestrian desire lines in clearly visible, straight paths.*

The crosswalk in this photo does not follow a straight path through the intersection. This not only increases crosswalk length, increasing exposure of pedestrians, but it also is difficult for pedestrians with visual impairments to follow the intended crosswalk path. The RSA team may suggest repainting the crosswalk straight across the intersection using continental or ladder markings or place a refuge island between the right turn and through lanes.

B.9 Signals

B.9.1 Are pedestrian signal heads provided and adequate?

Pedestrian signal heads provide important guidance to assist pedestrians in crossing an intersection safely. At intersections without pedestrian signal heads, pedestrians must rely on vehicle signals that do not accommodate pedestrian clearance requirements (which are substantially longer than vehicle clearance intervals). Furthermore, traffic signals may include complex phasing with traffic movements (such as lagging left turn movements) that pedestrians do not anticipate.

Typically, pedestrians benefit from pedestrian signal heads at signalized locations. Pedestrian signal phasing may need no activation or may be activated using pedestrian detectors (in which case push buttons are not necessary), or may be activated by manual push buttons.

Pedestrian Signal Heads

Pedestrian signal heads should be easily visible to pedestrians. The RSA team should determine if the following may be issues with the signal head placement:

➤ Are pedestrian signal heads reasonably in line with pedestrian travel paths?

➤ Are pedestrian signal heads large enough to be clearly seen from the opposite side of the street?

➤ Is the pedestrian signal head clearly visible along the entire length of the crosswalk?

➤ Is the pedestrian signal head placed at an appropriate height (not too high or too low)?

➤ Does background commercial lighting compete with the pedestrian signal display or render it inconspicuous?

➤ Is there confusion with pedestrian signals at the two-stage crossings?

➤ Do street signs or landscaping obstruct the visibility of pedestrian signals?

Push Buttons

The RSA team should determine if the following may be issues with the push buttons:

➤ Are pedestrian push buttons placed in locations accessible to all pedestrians?

➤ Are push buttons placed in locations and oriented so that they clearly indicate the crossing to which they apply?

➤ Is signage needed to explain their function and use?

B.9.2 Are traffic and pedestrian signals timed so that wait times and crossing times are reasonable?

Signal timing that causes excessive delay for pedestrians increases the likelihood that they will choose to disobey the signal. There are two components of traffic signal timing that affect pedestrians: wait time (the interval between a pedestrian's arrival at the intersection and the start of the applicable green or WALK signal phase) and crossing and clearance time (the time available for a pedestrian to cross the street). The RSA team should consider the following when evaluating signal timing for pedestrians:

Wait Time

The wait time for a pedestrian is dependent upon the traffic signal cycle length and phasing. The longer the cycle length, the longer the average wait time for a pedestrian. Pedestrians often walk against the signal when the signal cycle length or activation interval is too long.

Crossing and Clearance Time

Pedestrian clearance intervals (typically the interval during which the flashing DON'T WALK display is shown) are often based on an assumed walking speed of 4 feet per second. However, many pedestrians move at considerably slower speeds, including elderly people, children, people with disabilities, and people using strollers. Roadway features may also affect walking speeds, such as grade (see prompt A.2.3).

Crossing times may not be adequate when pedestrians:

➤ Frequently are caught in the crosswalk when the pedestrian signal shows a steady DON'T WALK display.

➤ Consistently must hurry to cross the street before the signal changes.

B.9.3 Is there a problem because of an inconsistency in pedestrian actuation (or detection) types?

Use of different pedestrian signal actuation types (i.e., automatic detection, push button actuation, or no actuation) within a small geographic area or along a single corridor may cause pedestrian confusion. For example, pedestrians may not perceive the need to actuate a push button-actuated signal in an urban area where most other pedestrian signals require no actuation. When a push button-actuated pedestrian signal is not activated, pedestrians may not receive a WALK display and may attempt to cross without the pedestrian signal. The RSA team should evaluate the consistency of pedestrian signal actuation and its effect on pedestrian safety.

B.9.4 Are all pedestrian signals and push buttons functioning correctly and safely?

For RSAs of existing facilities, the RSA team should verify that all pedestrian signals and push buttons are functioning properly. The RSA team should evaluate the following:

➤ Do all phases of the pedestrian signal light up properly?

➤ If an audible pedestrian signal is provided, do all audible signals operate?

➤ If a countdown signal is present, does the countdown skip numbers (especially with the onset of an emergency pre-empted signal phase)?

Push Buttons

> Is the push button properly attached to a pole?

> Is the push button operational? The RSA team should activate each push button to observe whether it calls a WALK phase.

> If an audible and/or tactile pedestrian push button is provided, are these features operational?

> Is the push button inaccessible due to poor sidewalk maintenance or poorly maintained landscaping?

B.9.5 Are ADA accessible push buttons provided and properly located?

The RSA team should determine if all signal push buttons, including those on medians and pedestrian refuge islands, are placed in locations accessible to all users. The team should consider the following:

> Is the activation button for a pedestrian signal located in a place that is easily found and reached by all users, including mobility- and vision-impaired pedestrians?

> Is access to the push button obstructed by street furniture, landscaping, bus shelters, or moveable obstructions such as newspaper boxes?

> Are they located along pedestrian desire lines (i.e., does a pedestrian need to change their direction of travel or backtrack to reach a push button)?

Pedestrian push buttons may be placed in locations that are far from the pedestrian crossing, which may discourage push button use and cause pedestrians not to notice if a push button is present.

RSA Examples

Location of pedestrian push buttons: *Push buttons may be placed in locations where the crossing they control is unclear, or placed in positions where they cannot be used by all pedestrians.* RSAs of new facilities should include a field review of pedestrian signal heads (which should be properly mounted and oriented) and push buttons (which should be located so that they are readily seen, convenient to use, and accessible to all users).

This photograph shows a pedestrian push button inconveniently located about a foot off the ground. In addition to being awkward to activate, the push button may be hidden by growing vegetation, damaged by mowing equipment, or covered by snow.

These push buttons appear to control the same crossing. Pedestrians may fail to use the correct push button for the desired crossing which may result in pedestrians crossing without a WALK signal.

This photo shows a long pedestrian crossing on a major arterial with a median push button. The timing was set to allow most people to be able to cross the entire street. For those who needed extra time to cross, a push button was provided midblock (circled), but is inaccessible to pedestrians with mobility impairments. This pedestrian, who was still in the crosswalk when the pedestrian crossing phase was over, was unable to activate the pedestrian push button.

C. PARKING AREAS/ADJACENT DEVELOPMENTS

Overview

The prompts in this section provide a more detailed description of some of the specific issues that may be present in parking areas and adjacent developments, which often are privately owned. The design of parking areas and adjacent developments can significantly affect pedestrian safety and the ability to access commercial, civic, or other spaces. Pedestrians may avoid a designated crossing or path because the connection to a parking area or adjacent development is perceived as dangerous or is nonexistent. Proper planning and design can reduce conflicts with automobiles for pedestrians walking through parking lots, accessing developments adjacent to the street or pedestrian network, or crossing driveways that connect parking lots to the street.

Transportation facility designs are sometimes second to architectural designs in parking areas and adjacent developments. These transportation facilities often favor vehicular traffic and do not always apply standard roadway design, signing, and pavement marking principles. Pedestrian facilities may be scarce, situated away from pedestrian desire lines, or designed without proper consideration for pedestrian safety. The driving task is complicated by drivers looking at stores and trying to find parking spaces, putting pedestrians at higher risk for being hit by distracted drivers in these areas. These conditions may promote unsafe pedestrian and motorist behaviors.

The section numbers correspond to the numbers found in the prompt lists. **Many of the prompts applicable to streets and at crossings (Sections A and B) will apply to these facilities and should also be consulted.**

C.1 Presence, Design, and Placement

C.1.1 Do sidewalks/paths connect the street and adjacent land uses?

Pedestrian facilities between the street and adjacent developments/parking areas are sometimes neglected. Pedestrian destinations, such as commercial, institutional, and office buildings, should have delineated walkways between the major entrance(s) and the street. Schools should have clearly marked pathways that provide direct access between sidewalks and the entrance so that students do not have to cut across drop-off/pickup lanes.

C.1.2 Are the sidewalks/paths designed appropriately?

The RSA team should ensure pedestrian facilities are designed to accommodate existing and future demands by considering the following:

> ➤ Are sidewalks or paths wide enough for existing or anticipated peak pedestrian volumes and types?

> ➤ Are sidewalks or paths placed so that they are protected from vehicles and other modes of travel?

> ➤ Are appropriate crossings provided?

C.1.3 Are buildings entrances located and designed to be obvious and easily accessible to pedestrians?

Paths to entrances should be reasonably direct, to encourage their use. When building entrances are not obvious, pedestrians may travel longer distances to find the entrance, potentially increasing their exposure to conflicts with other traffic modes. Inaccessible entrances may require pedestrians with disabilities to take longer paths, as well as paths that conflict with other traffic modes.

RSA Examples

Absence of pedestrian facilities: Building arrangements often require pedestrians to take awkward paths though parking lots. Many large commercial parking areas are designed with only vehicular traffic in mind, and have no marked travel paths for pedestrians needing to cross the parking lot or walk to and from their vehicles or transit stops. Parking lots are frequently characterized by distracted drivers, erratic vehicle maneuvers (including backing), and uncontrolled intersections, all of which increase the risk to pedestrians walking on the roadway.

Pedestrians in the parking lot of a shopping mall are walking in the roadway where they may conflict with vehicles. The absence of sidewalks or clear pedestrian pathways exposes pedestrians to the risk of collision with drivers who are often distracted by the need to find a parking spot.

Pedestrian facilities should be provided to accommodate pedestrian demand and desire lines. In this photograph, pedestrians have worn a direct path between a parking area and a large pedestrian generator. No roadway crossing facilities are provided for this "unofficial" pathway, with the result that pedestrians using it must cross an unlighted, curved interchange ramp access where drivers may not expect pedestrians.

C.2 Quality, Condition, and Obstructions

C.2.1 Do parked vehicles obstruct pedestrian paths?

Legally or illegally parked vehicles may obstruct pedestrian pathways, including marked crosswalks. Obstruction of pedestrian pathways by parked vehicles often occurs:

> ➤ Where parking supply falls short of demand, so drivers park in any available area.

> ➤ Near major building accesses, where vehicles parked for passenger pickup/drop-off or for convenience interfere with pedestrians entering and exiting the building.

> ➤ Where parking areas are too close to pedestrian facilities, with the result that vehicle overhangs intrude on pedestrian pathways.

> ➤ Where parking facilities are inconvenient, causing drivers to park in unoccupied or more convenient areas reserved for pedestrian use.

The RSA team should evaluate parking generators during periods of peak parking demand on an RSA of an existing facility.

Vehicles can form obstructions to pedestrians. Statutes and regulations are required to support enforcement of policies such as no parking on sidewalks. Here an automobile dealer used the sidewalk to store excess vehicle inventory.

RSA Example

Drivers may park where their vehicles obstruct pedestrian facilities: *Parked or waiting vehicles may partly or entirely obstruct pedestrian facilities such as sidewalks and crosswalks. Motorists may knowingly or unknowingly block pedestrian paths. When pedestrian paths are blocked, pedestrians may take paths that put them in conflict with vehicular traffic.*

Vehicle overhangs partly block a sidewalk. The sidewalk width appears to still be sufficient to accommodate a wheelchair, but some of the pedestrians walking in a group have entered the roadway at the narrowed part of the sidewalk. The RSA team may suggest placing parking stops and signs at the front of the parking space to encourage drivers to pull completely into parking spaces.

C.3 Continuity and Connectivity

C.3.1 Are pedestrian facilities continuous? Do they provide adequate connections for pedestrian traffic?

Pedestrians accessing a destination may travel by car, transit, or entirely on foot. The pedestrian network should provide a continuous pathway for pedestrians accessing the destination by these modes. Continuity should be provided:

> ➤ Along the pedestrian facilities connecting areas within the destination (including between areas used for transit, parking, and pickup/drop-off).
> ➤ To connect the destination with adjacent developments.
> ➤ To connect the destination with the adjacent transportation network.

C.3.2 Are transitions of pedestrian facilities between developments/projects adequate?

Pedestrian transitions between private developments, and between a private development and the public right of way, are sometimes disregarded. The RSA team should evaluate the adequacy of pedestrian facilities at transitional locations at all phases of development to ensure they are easily accessible to all users, including those with visual and mobility disabilities.

RSA Examples

Transition areas between projects:
The absence of smooth transitions is sometimes a particular problem for private pedestrian facilities. As a result, pedestrians may have no safe and accessible path between developments, which can result in pedestrians taking paths that will put them into conflict with vehicles.

In this photograph there is an abrupt transition between the sidewalk serving this public bus stop and the adjacent private sidewalk. Pedestrians with mobility impairments will have a difficult time traveling between the bus stop and the adjacent development and may have to travel in the street where motorists may not expect to encounter them.

RSA Examples (continued)

Poor connectivity & signage: *Pedestrians should be provided clear, direct paths that minimize exposure.* Signage can be used to help clearly indicate these paths. A well-signed facility alone is not enough to get pedestrians to properly use sidewalks and other facilities; the design must also include logical travel paths that lead conveniently to major destinations.

A covered walkway has been provided to connect a major shopping center and transit station, but the walkway does not follow pedestrian desire lines. As a result, pedestrians frequently shortcut through the shopping center parking lot (as shown in the photograph), where no designated pedestrian pathway is available.

This shopping facility has a frontage road parallel to a busy, arterial highway. Pedestrian facilities and signage creates a circuitous route, which does not follow pedestrian desire lines and puts pedestrians in conflict with traffic on the frontage road. As is seen in this photograph, pedestrians will often ignore the pedestrian facilities and walk instead in the frontage road closer to the commercial establishments.

An absence of continuity is apparent in this photograph, where a marked pedestrian crosswalk over a circulating road in a commercial development ends in a landscaped area. No connecting walkway is provided, so pedestrians must walk in the street.

RSA Examples (continued)

Good connectivity of pedestrian facilities: *A well-designed system of sidewalks with ramps connecting even to the farthest parking spaces provides clearly separated, safe paths for pedestrians.*

This parking lot for an event center effectively separates vehicle and pedestrian traffic. People parking in any aisle have a fully accessible sidewalk at the end of the aisle leading directly to the main facility building. Landscaping from the sidewalk to the parking lot is well designed, as it not only does not block visibility of pedestrians, but also channels them to cross at aisles. The RSA team may suggest adding sidewalk lighting and marked crosswalks at the pedestrian access points to enhance pedestrian conspicuity.

Accessibility for all pedestrians: *Parking areas should accommodate all pedestrians. Although pedestrians with disabilities are typically accommodated in close-in parking stalls, they may be required to park in non-designated stalls if designated stalls are occupied or if they have no authorization to use them (such as if they are temporarily disabled).*

A pedestrian crosswalk with a curb ramp is provided to help direct pedestrians through a commercial parking area to a sidewalk. However, the sidewalk width is reduced to about 18 inches where an electrical box and protective bollards are located. Pedestrians unable to pass in the narrow width (especially those pushing strollers, in wheelchairs, or carrying packages) must walk in the parking lot, where they risk conflicting with vehicles. The obstruction may also present an obstacle for a visually impaired pedestrian. The RSA team may suggest widening the sidewalk around the transformer.

C.5 Visibility

The presence of numerous vehicles and pedestrians operating in close proximity to each other makes visibility especially important in parking areas.

C.5.1 Are visibility and sight distance adequate?

Pedestrian safety is improved when drivers and pedestrians have clear and unobstructed views of each other in and on the approaches to areas where they may conflict. The RSA team should observe potential conflict points to assess whether visibility of both vehicles and pedestrians is adequate, and whether clear and unobstructed sightlines are maintained.

Obstructions may reduce sightlines between pedestrians and drivers in parking areas and near driveways. Sightline obstructions may be permanent, seasonal, or transient, and might include:

> Hard and soft landscaping features, such as trees, bushes, ornamental plants, decorative walls/fences, and fountains.

> Parked vehicles and loading/unloading vehicles.

> Columns and other architectural elements.

> Transit shelters.

> Commercial signing.

> Temporary or seasonal displays, such as holiday decorations.

> Outdoor retail activities, such as food stands, merchandise displays, or sidewalk dining areas.

Large columns obstruct sightlines between pedestrians approaching marked crosswalks and vehicles exiting a parking area. The columns also limit the sidewalk width.

Adequate visibility of vehicles and pedestrians promotes drivers' and pedestrians' awareness of each other. The RSA team should observe pedestrian facilities under varying weather and lighting conditions to assess:

> The need for, or adequacy of, night-time lighting.

> The visibility of pedestrians and vehicles in areas affected by strong shadows (such as near the entry to a covered parking area).

> The impact of commercial elements such as bright lighting or distracting displays.

See Section A.6 for questions related to visibility at driveways that apply to sidewalks and walkways at off-site or parking lot locations.

Vehicles in pull-in parking stalls immediately adjacent to a marked crosswalk obstruct sightlines between circulating vehicles and pedestrians in and approaching the crosswalk. The obstruction is transient, since sightlines would improve when the stalls are unoccupied. In addition to obstructing sightlines, vehicles backing out of the stalls may conflict with pedestrians in the crosswalk.

RSA Examples

Conflicts with backing vehicles: *Pedestrians should be directed away from areas where they may conflict with vehicles entering and exiting parking spaces, especially backing vehicles.* The risk of collision is increased where tall vehicles, such as trucks or SUVs, block sightlines for a driver backing out of an adjacent stall.

A pedestrian walkway is marked through a major truck terminal. The walkway is well marked, and pedestrians in this facility are required to wear high visibility clothing. However, pedestrian crossings are long and unlit, and pedestrians are subject to conflicts from a variety of through and turning movements by vehicles approaching from several directions. A higher level of visibility for pedestrian crosswalks, and more positive measures to ensure that drivers are aware of crosswalk location and occupancy, would improve pedestrian safety.

The intended path for pedestrians in this photograph is marked with ladder style pavement markings that put pedestrians directly in the path of backing vehicles. Pedestrians may feel a false degree of safety walking in a marked path, which cannot be seen by a backing motorist. This path would be safer if placed on the other side of the parking area (off to the right side of the photo).

Driver distraction: Drivers entering and exiting a parking facility may be distracted by wayfinding or payment activities. Distracted drivers may fail to anticipate pedestrians, increasing the risk of a pedestrian/vehicle conflict. In addition, drivers entering or exiting a covered parking area (such as a parking garage) may fail to see pedestrians as their vision adjusts to darker or brighter conditions. Pedestrian accesses and pathways should be clearly marked, well separated and protected from traffic, and easily accessible to pedestrians.

A pedestrian enters an underground parking facility using the vehicle driveway, rather than an indoor pedestrian elevator that was not well signed from the street. Drivers entering or exiting the parking facility, where sightlines are restricted and lighting is limited, may fail to anticipate a pedestrian in the driveway.

C.6. Access Management

C.6.1 Are travel paths for pedestrians and other vehicle modes clearly defined at access openings?

Access points leading to and from parking areas should effectively direct entering and exiting vehicles along well-defined paths to minimize interference with pedestrians. Uncontrolled accesses that are poorly defined may generate issues associated with:

> **Higher speeds**–Wide and/or poorly delineated accesses may encourage higher speeds among entering and exiting drivers. A wide access area may be used to accelerate or decelerate when entering or leaving the adjacent road. High speeds may increase the risk and severity of a pedestrian collision.

> **Driver and pedestrian expectancy**–Wide and/or poorly delineated accesses provide little guidance to drivers concerning the appropriate place to enter or exit a property to limit interference with pedestrians crossing the access point or walking in the parking area. As a result, the potential for conflict is increased, increasing the risk of a pedestrian crash.

A wide driveway with no defined entry or exit points exposes pedestrians on the sidewalk to interference from drivers accessing the commercial premises over a large, undefined area. Drivers can enter or leave the driveway at a shallow angle, and consequently at a high speed, increasing the risk of collision with pedestrians on the sidewalk or in the parking area.

C.6.2 Do drivers look for and yield to pedestrians when turning into and out of driveways?

Drivers entering and exiting a driveway have a high driver workload, since they must monitor traffic on the main road, traffic in the driveway or parking area, pedestrians crossing the driveway, and pedestrians in the parking area. Since pedestrian visibility is generally limited relative to vehicle visibility, drivers may fail to observe pedestrians, increasing the risk of conflicts. Several factors may increase the risk and severity of pedestrian-vehicle conflicts:

- ➤ High vehicle and/or pedestrian volumes (including recurring peaks, such as near a school or theatre).

- ➤ High volumes or speeds on the through road that focus drivers' attention on avoiding traffic (rather than pedestrian) conflicts.

- ➤ Sightline obstructions or poor night-time lighting that limits drivers' view of pedestrians.

C.7 Traffic Characteristics

C.7.1 Does pedestrian or driver behavior increase the risk of a pedestrian collision?

Drivers and pedestrians may behave differently in parking areas, where pedestrians and vehicles mix more freely, speeds are often low, and there is typically no enforcement. The RSA team may observe behavior issues such as:

- ➤ **Vehicle speed**–Is traffic operating at inappropriately high speeds? If so, what elements (such as wide lanes, generous driveway geometry, or long aisles) may contribute to higher speeds?

- ➤ **Pedestrians in travel lanes**–Do pedestrians typically walk in vehicle travel lanes? If so, the RSA Team may use the prompts in this section to assess whether adequate pedestrian facilities are provided.

- ➤ **Disregard for traffic controls**–Do drivers or pedestrians disregard traffic control devices such as signs and pavement markings? If so, the RSA team may consider whether the non-standard design and installation of these devices is an issue, and whether devices are adequately maintained.

Motorists exiting driveways are often focused on finding gaps in traffic rather than pedestrians walking along the street.

C.7.2 Are buses, cars, bicycles, and pedestrians separated on the site and provided with their own designated areas for travel?

Pedestrian conflicts with motor vehicles should be minimized by providing appropriate sidewalks and crossing facilities, especially at schools. Several issues that the RSA team should consider are:

> Are drop-off and pickup zones separated from walking routes?

> Is a pedestrian network provided so that pedestrians do not have to walk for extended distances in parking lanes or circulating aisles?

> Do sidewalks lead in a reasonably direct and efficient manner to all the destinations that pedestrians want to access?

C.8 Signs and Pavement Markings

C.8.1 Are travel paths and crossing points for pedestrians properly signed and/or marked?

The RSA team should assess signs and pavement markings to confirm that they provide adequate guidance and warning to drivers and pedestrians in and on the approaches to potential conflict points. Consideration should be given to:

> **Use of appropriate signs and pavement markings**–A range of standard signs and pavement markings can be used to provide guidance and warning to drivers on the approach to crosswalks. Standard signs and markings, such as STOP signs, pedestrian crossing signs, and crosswalk markings are generally more easily recognized and understood by drivers, and are consequently preferable to non-standard traffic signs and markings in parking areas.

> **Proper installation of signs and pavement markings**–Appropriate installation promotes the visibility and conspicuity of signs and pavement markings. Signs should be installed at an appropriate height and lateral offset, and should not be obstructed by columns, landscaping, stopped or parked vehicles, or other obstructions. Adjacent commercial signing, lighting, or displays should not distract drivers' attention from pedestrian signage. Signing and pavement markings should be installed where they are clearly visible on the vehicle to the intended user.

> **Maintenance of existing signs and pavement markings**–On RSAs of existing facilities, the RSA team should observe existing signs and pavement markings for damage, fading, and wearing.

The RSA team may consult the MUTCD (Parts 2 and 3) for guidance on the types, proper use, and correct installation of standard pedestrian-related signs and markings.

In addition to vehicle signs and markings, pedestrian signing may be reviewed. Pedestrian signing may be necessary to guide pedestrians (for example, to transit facilities, crossing locations, or specific destinations), or warn pedestrians of potential conflict points.

RSA Example

Adequate signing and pavement marking: *Signing and pavement markings should be properly designed and implemented in parking areas.* Signs and pavement markings in parking lots often fail to follow requirements in the *Manual of Uniform Traffic Control Devices (MUTCD)* since they are not on public roads. Consequently, signs and markings may be missing, misplaced, or contradictory. Since drivers expect consistency in the placement and meaning of signs and pavement markings, whether they are in a public road or parking area, signs and pavement markings should follow MUTCD guidelines in parking areas as well as public roads.

Inappropriate pavement markings may increase the risk of pedestrian collision. The stop bar has been placed beyond the brick crosswalk in the center of the photo, with the result that vehicles stop in the crosswalk. A second crosswalk has been painted beyond the stop bar in an attempt to mitigate the situation, but the painted crosswalk has no curb ramps and is consequently less accessible to pedestrians in wheelchairs, scooters, or pushing strollers.

D. TRANSIT

Overview

The prompts in this section are intended to help the RSA team identify pedestrian safety problems at transit and school bus stops. Because buses represent the most common type of transit in most U.S. jurisdictions this section focuses on bus transit issues (including school bus service), but some of the principles will apply for light rail service provided on streets.

The RSA team should also understand the context in which each of these is sited when assessing safety and providing suggestions for improvement. Light rail service may change the least whereas school bus stops may change most frequently.

Potential issues that may arise from connecting pedestrian facilities such as sidewalks and adjacent crossings are discussed in Sections A and B, and transit-specific issues on these facilities will be described and reinforced in this section. The section numbers correspond to the numbers found in the prompt lists.

D.1 Presence, Design, and Placement

D.1.1 Are bus stops sited properly?

Bus stops should be located next to pedestrian traffic generators or along pedestrian desire lines. When they are not, pedestrians may take unsafe paths to reach transit stops or neglect to pay adequate attention to traffic. Potential issues the RSA team should consider when evaluating the placement of transit stops include the following:

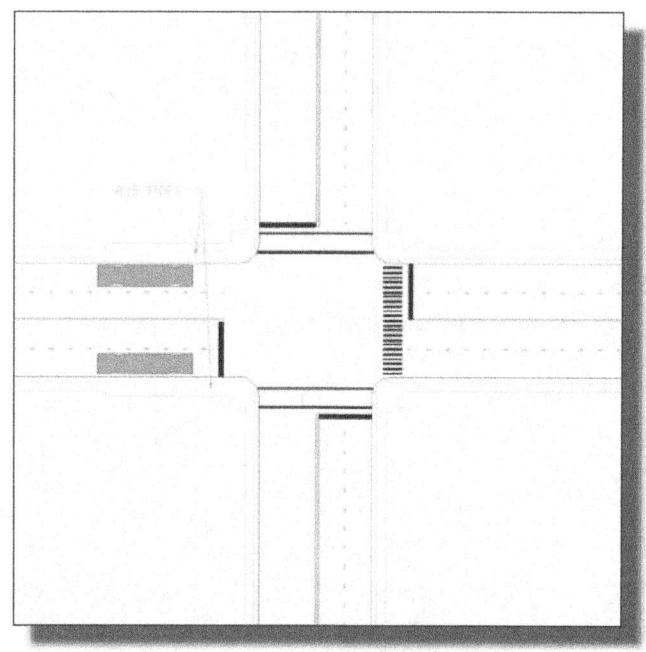

> **Far-side stops**–At busy intersections bus stops are often placed after the intersection ("far-side"), so that alighting passengers do not cross in front of the bus. However, it is important to position the bus stop far enough from the intersection so that buses do not block the intersection or crosswalk.

> **Near-side stops**–If transit stops are located before the intersection ("near side"), alighting passengers may be at risk if they cross the street in front of the vehicle since they may be outside of the driver's sightlines.

> **Midblock**–Midblock transit stops can encourage passengers to cross at unmarked midblock crossings, violating driver expectancy.

Bus stops may be sited without adequate consideration of pedestrian desire lines. The illustration above shows a poor placement of bus stops with respect to pedestrian crossings. Pedestrians using transit would be required to cross three intersection legs to reach the opposite side of the street.

D.1.2 Are safe pedestrian crossings convenient for transit and school bus users?

The RSA team should consider the following when determining if crossings are placed conveniently for pedestrians:

➤ Are crossings located reasonably close to school bus and transit stops?

➤ If the bus stop is near an intersection with marked crosswalks, is there a crosswalk on the approach closest to the bus stop, or are pedestrians required to cross three legs of a four leg intersection to reach the opposite side of the street?

To evaluate the crossing itself, the RSA team should review the prompt list in *Section B: Crossings.*

D.1.3 Is sight distance to bus stops adequate?

Sufficient stopping sight distance should be available on the approaches to school bus and transit stops, since the stops can generate substantial pedestrian crossing volumes. Stopping sight distance may meet required AASHTO policy values, but due to the limited visibility of pedestrians (especially child pedestrians and during low-light conditions) and potential to violate drivers' expectations, may be insufficient. Areas of particular concern include crest vertical curves and horizontal curves, where sight distance is often limited.

Pedestrians crossing the street to reach the bus stop circled in the photograph above will be hidden by the crest of the vertical curve.

The RSA team should consider the placement of the bus stop in low-density and rural areas where minimum geometric standards may not be consistently met or maintained, and pedestrians are less frequent.

D.1.4. Are shelters appropriately designed and placed for pedestrian safety and convenience?

The RSA team should evaluate the placement of bus shelters, including how they may affect pedestrian traffic. The team should consider the following conditions:

➤ Are the shelter and/or paved area large enough to accommodate waiting riders?

➤ Could a person using a wheelchair fit completely under the shelter?

➤ Can a pedestrian in a wheelchair fit between the shelter and the bus doors when the bus doors are opened?

➤ Can all users enter and exit the shelter without interfering with motor vehicle traffic, cyclists, or through pedestrian traffic?

➤ Is the shelter close enough to the curb that bus drivers easily notice waiting passengers, especially at night?

➢ Does the shelter obstruct the sidewalk or reduce its usable width so that pedestrians in wheelchairs, scooters, or pushing strollers may be unable to pass on the sidewalk?

➢ Will pedestrians waiting in shelter be splashed by approaching buses during rainy/ inclement weather?

Photo on left by PBIC.

The photo on the left illustrates a bus stop with a setback over 8 feet, facilitating access by all pedestrians (note that however the fire hydrant may limit access). The photo on the right shows a bus stop with a setback of less than 5 feet. Persons in a wheelchair would have a difficult time accessing this bus stop.

RSA Example

Location of transit stops: *Transit stops may interfere with pedestrian pathways or facilities.* Transit facilities are typically provided in conjunction with pedestrian facilities, since transit riders must walk to and from the transit stop. The risk of pedestrian collisions may increase if pedestrian pathways (marked or reflecting pedestrian desire lines) conflict with bus movements, particularly when pedestrians walk close to accelerating or turning transit vehicles, or pass between queued transit vehicles. Adequate sightlines, unobstructed by waiting transit vehicles or facilities (such as bus shelters), should always be maintained between pedestrians and drivers. Clear and unobstructed pedestrian pathways should be provided, and unsafe pedestrian movements should be discouraged.

The picture shows a bus blocking the crosswalk. This not only prevents pedestrians from using the crosswalk, but also presents a hazard to people alighting the bus. Transit riders would not be able to tell where to cross the street. The RSA team may suggest provided a clearly marked bus stop in front of the crosswalk.

D.2 Quality, Condition, and Obstructions

D.2.1 Is the seating area at a safe and comfortable distance from vehicle and bicycle lanes?

The RSA team should evaluate the placement of seating and how it may affect pedestrian use and safety. Seating that is too close to the curb may discourage transit use, or cause pedestrians to wait in areas that may put them in conflict with vehicles, bicyclists, or other pedestrians. The team should consider the following conditions:

- ➤ Can a pedestrian in a wheelchair fit between the bench and the bus doors when opened?
- ➤ Can all users use the seating area without interfering with motor vehicle traffic, cyclists, or through pedestrian traffic?
- ➤ Will pedestrians waiting at the seating area be splashed by approaching buses during rain/inclement weather?

D.2.2 Do seats (or persons sitting on them) obstruct the sidewalk or reduce its usable width?

Seating (as well as persons occupying the seats) should not obstruct pedestrians walking on the sidewalk, particularly pedestrians in wheelchairs, scooters, or pushing strollers.

Additional potential issues the RSA team should look for include:

- ➤ Do seats (or persons sitting on them) pose a hazard to blind pedestrians?
- ➤ Do seats (or persons sitting on them) reduce usable width due to the presence of trees, signal cabinets, parked cars, or other obstructions?

D.2.3 Is a sufficient landing area provided to accommodate waiting passengers, boarding/ alighting passengers, and through/bypassing pedestrian traffic at peak times?

The RSA team should determine whether there is sufficient landing area at the bus stop to accommodate three groups during peak times: passengers boarding and alighting the bus, passengers waiting for other buses, and pedestrians walking past the bus stop. If the landing area is not sufficient, pedestrians (especially disabled pedestrians) may have difficulty boarding, alighting, or passing through the waiting crowd, which may result in pedestrians bypassing the area.

People waiting for the bus on this narrow sidewalk completely block access for someone passing in a wheelchair.

D.2.4 Is the landing area paved and free of problems such as uneven surfaces, standing water, or steep slopes?

A well-maintained, level paved surface provides secure footing for passengers stepping into and out

The landing area at a bus stop is the area where waiting passengers stand, and the surface that passengers exiting the bus step onto.

of transit and school buses, and a secure area for wheelchairs and strollers entering and exiting a bus. Poorly maintained walking surfaces (including those with uneven surfaces, standing water, ice, or steep slopes) generate tripping or slipping hazards, and can obstruct or endanger passengers, particularly those with visual or mobility impairments. Landings that slope toward the street can cause strollers and wheelchairs to roll into the street.

Prompt A.2 describes sidewalk conditions that also apply to transit stops.

D.2.5 Is the sidewalk free of temporary/permanent obstructions that constrict its width or block access to the bus stop?

A landing area with significant slopes in any direction is a safety concern, especially for people with disabilities or using strollers.

The RSA team should determine whether there are any temporary or permanent obstructions to accessing transit and school bus stops (both bus ingress and egress) and bus shelters. Potential issues to consider include:

> Do obstructions pose risks for persons with visual impairments?

> For all potential users, do street furniture and utilities (such as landscaping, newspaper boxes, or fire hydrants) obstruct:
  ▷ Access to the bus stop or bus shelter?
  ▷ Entry or exit doors on the bus?

> Could passengers (especially those with vision impairments) have difficulty in seeing bus stops due to obstructions such as newspaper boxes, landscaping, etc?

See also prompt A.2.2 on obstructions that applies to sidewalks.

The photo on the left shows access to a bus stop (in the distance) obstructed by a telephone pole. Access to the bus shelter on the right is inhibited due to a missing connection between the sidewalk and the bus shelter landing.

RSA Examples

Adequate facilities for riders at transit facilities: *Transit facilities should be sufficient to allow passengers to enter, exit, or wait for transit vehicles in comfort and without interfering with vehicle, bicycle, or pedestrian traffic.* Pedestrians waiting for the bus frequently block the sidewalk because the waiting area is not large enough to meet demand. This may cause pedestrians to walk around people waiting and into or near the street, increasing conflicts and the risk of a collision between a vehicle (especially a bus) and a pedestrian.

Transit riders waiting for a bus block the sidewalk. Pedestrians may enter the roadway to bypass the waiting passengers, resulting in conflicts with vehicles or bicycles in the curb lane. The RSA team may suggest extending the curb at this location to provide adequate space for waiting passengers. The curb extension can be integrated with the on street parking.

Bus stops on islands with inadequate pedestrian facilities: Bus stops should be sufficient to allow passengers to enter, exit, or wait for transit vehicles in comfort and without interfering with vehicle, bicycle, or pedestrian traffic.

A transit stop is located on a 3' wide channelizing island (separating through and left turning traffic) on a major urban arterial. Traffic passes on both sides of the island. Riders waiting for a bus have a limited space in which to queue, and riders exiting a bus have a narrow space in which to alight and wait to cross the travel lanes. Buses must load and unload passengers from this narrow island adjacent to moving traffic.

A bus stop is located on a right turn channelizing island. Traffic passes on both sides of the island. Riders waiting for a bus have limited space in which to queue. Since the island is too short to accommodate riders exiting a bus by the rear door, riders must enter and exit buses by the front door only. Consequently, entering and exiting passengers must all be accommodated in a very limited space in, rather than at the side of, the roadway.

D.3 Continuity and Connectivity

D.3.1. Is the nearest crossing opportunity free of potential hazards for pedestrians?

An appropriate level of control, signing, and marking should be provided at crossings near transit stops. On a low-speed, low-volume, neighborhood street, a nearby intersection with no marked crosswalks and no traffic signal may be an appropriate street crossing. The same level of control would not be adequate on a higher-speed or higher-volume road. Potential issues related to nearby crossing opportunities include:

> Sightline obstructions due to roadway geometry (i.e., hills, horizontal curves, etc.).

> Steep grades or cross slopes in or on the approaches to the crossings.

> Presence of on-street parking that could obstruct sightlines near the crossings.

> Proximity to at-grade rail crossings.

> Location of the crosswalk and design of curb ramps.

> Dangerous traffic conditions, such as high speeds, a high proportion of turning vehicles, or a substantial proportion of heavy vehicles.

D.3.2 Are transit and school bus stops part of a continuous network of pedestrian facilities?

The RSA team should evaluate the adequacy of pedestrian facilities surrounding a transit or school bus stop. Missing or non-continuous sidewalks (or walkable shoulders) effectively reduces the bus stop service area for many people, especially for children, the elderly and persons with disabilities. Missing or non-continuous sidewalks may cause pedestrians to walk on the road to reach the bus stop.

D.3.3 Are transit and school bus stops maintained during periods of inclement weather?

Waiting and landing areas at transit and school bus stops may be affected by rain, snow, or ice. Bus stop facilities that cannot accommodate pedestrians under these conditions may be unusable, with the result that bus drivers and riders may prefer to use adjacent areas that are not designed for transit use for waiting, boarding, and alighting. The RSA team should determine the following:

> Could snow banks from passing snow plows obstruct passengers attempting to board or alight a bus?

> Could water or ice accumulate in or near the landing area where passengers approach, board, or alight the bus?

> Are sidewalks, curb ramps, and crosswalks clear of snow?

> Is the boarding or landing area sloped or uneven, increasing the risk that passengers may slip under snowy or icy conditions as they enter or exit the bus?

RSA Examples

Bus stop connectivity: *Transition areas from walkable shoulders to a sidewalk may be inadequate.* Transitions that are not clear may result in pedestrians taking erratic paths which may violate driver expectancy.

The bus stop waiting pad pictured does not provide an accessible ramp, making it difficult for people with mobility restrictions to reach the waiting pad. As a result pedestrians with mobility restrictions may take unexpected paths or wait in the shoulder, potentially interfering with bus stop traffic operations and cyclists. The RSA team may suggest installing an accessible ramp.

A well used bus stop that serves five bus routes is accessed by an unpaved footpath. The unpaved path may be difficult for pedestrians with disabilities to navigate, particularly when it is wet or icy. The waiting area at the bus stop is similarly unpaved, and pedestrians entering or exiting a bus must step onto the grassy strip at left, which may not provide secure footing (especially when wet). Persons using wheelchairs or strollers may also find it difficult to board or alight the bus because of the grassy strip.

Absence of a sidewalk: *Since riders must sidewalk to and from transit stops, adequate sidewalks should be provided adjacent to transit facilities.* Sidewalks should be wide enough to accommodate bus queues and through pedestrian traffic at the same time, as well as pedestrian surges associated with an unloading bus.

This pedestrian is walking in a busy street after alighting the bus. The fact that there is no formal walk or paved path along the street and that the right lane is wide enough for a vehicle to pass, probably were key factors in her decision to walk in the street. The RSA team may suggest placing a sidewalk along the street.

D.4 Lighting

D.4.1 Are access ways to transit and school bus facilities well-lit to accommodate early-morning, late-afternoon, and evening transit riders?

The RSA team should determine if school bus stops and transit stops, along with their approaches, have sufficient lighting for pedestrians walking to and from and waiting at the stop. Lighting conditions at transit stops should be evaluated at night. Specifically, the RSA team should evaluate the following:

> ➤ Is lighting adequate to illuminate pedestrians waiting at the stop so that they can be seen by drivers (including bus drivers) and cyclists?

> ➤ Does lighting illuminate nearby crossing points for pedestrians walking to and from the stop?

> ➤ Does lighting illuminate pedestrian pathways accessing the bus stop, so that pedestrians can see potential obstructions or uneven pavement on the path?

> ➤ Do trees or buildings reduce the amount of light that actually reaches the stop (see prompt A.4)?

D.5 Visibility

D.5.1. Are open sight lines maintained between approaching buses and passenger waiting and loading areas?

The RSA team should determine whether bus drivers and passengers waiting at transit and school bus stops can easily see each other. Several potential issues to consider are:

> ➤ Do bus drivers have a clear sight line to the bus stop or shelter, so that they have sufficient time to see and stop for passengers?

> ➤ Do passengers waiting at the bus stop and in the shelter have sufficient time to see and hail the bus, especially at transit or school bus stops serving more than one route?

> ➤ Are bus shelters transparent and well lit?

> ➤ Does the shelter (empty or occupied) obstruct sightlines at an intersection or driveway for drivers, cyclists, or through pedestrians?

> ➤ Does the shelter obstruct roadway signing?

If sightlines are obstructed, bus drivers may stop abruptly when waiting passengers become visible, or passengers may wait in or close to the road for better visibility, where they may conflict with drivers and cyclists.

D.7 Traffic Characteristics

D.7.1 Do pedestrians entering and leaving buses conflict with cars, bicycles, or other pedestrians?

Passengers approaching and leaving buses may have to cross other pedestrian traffic on the sidewalk, cyclists (in bicycle lanes or on the sidewalk), or vehicle lanes. Conflicts with these other modes may result in injury. The risk of conflicts is increased by:

> **Poor sightlines**–Sightlines may be obstructed by parked vehicles (including other buses), bus shelter walls, or street furniture.

> **Higher speeds**–Motor vehicles, as well as cyclists in bicycle lanes or on the sidewalk, may be traveling a higher speeds, contributing the possible risk and severity of a collision with a pedestrian crossing their path.

School bus loading/unloading zones require particular attention, since children are typically more difficult to see, are less aware of traffic safety, and behave in a less predictable manner. School bus loading zones should be well separated from parent drop-off and pickup areas so that children do not cross vehicle paths.

In the photo on the left, buses stop in a no-parking area, while in the photo on the right, buses stop in a bus bay. Both stops effectively separate transit riders from other modes of travel.

D.8 Signs and Pavement Markings

D.8.1. Are appropriate signs and pavement markings provided for school bus and transit stops?

Signing should be adequate to help identify transit and school bus stops for all users, and potentially warn motorists of the possibility for pedestrians where they may not be expected. The RSA team should consider the following when evaluating signage for bus stops:

> The need for advance warning signs, especially in rural areas.

> The potential for pedestrian crossings.

> Parking regulations.

➤ Way finding, especially at schools.

➤ Transit service information.

The RSA team should also consider that overuse of signs may reduce overall sign effectiveness, so signing should reflect actual hazards or conditions that are likely to cause conflicts. Seasonal pedestrian peaks (such as near schools or recreational areas) may require temporary signing.

The RSA team should also determine whether bus stops have appropriate pavement markings, considering the experience or limitations of likely users. Potential issues the RSA team should look for include:

➤ Do bus stop and bus lane pavement markings alert motorists of the presence of pedestrians even when a bus is not present?

➤ Are stand-back lines, which are used frequently at schools, effective in helping pedestrians to know where to stand and keep them separated from bus traffic?

The photo shows an example of stand-back lines in a bus loading zone. The lines help direct pedestrians away from the curb when they are waiting or walking on the sidewalk. By increasing the distance between pedestrians and buses, the stand-back lines reduce the risk of collision involving buses arriving at or departing from the loading zone.

References:

1. National Highway Traffic Safety Administration (NHTSA), Dept. of Transportation (US), 2005 .*Traffic Safety Facts 2005: Annual Report.* http://www-nrd.nhtsa.dot.gov/pdf/nrd-30/NCSA/TSFAnn/TSF2005.pdf Washington, DC.

2. National Highway Traffic Safety Administration (NHTSA), Dept. of Transportation (US), 2005. *Traffic Safety Facts 2005: Pedestrians.* http://www-nrd.nhtsa.dot.gov/pdf/nrd-30/NCSA/TSF2005/810624.pdf Washington, DC.

3. Surface Transportation Policy Project. *Mean Streets: How Far Have We Come?* (2004). Available online at http://www.transact.org/library/reports_html/ms2004/exec_sum.asp, accessed October 4, 2006.

4. Chu, Xuehao, 2003. "The Fatality Risk of Walking in America: A Time-Based Comparative Approach." *Walk 21 (IV) Conference Proceedings.* Available online at http://www.americawalks.org/PDF_PAPE/Chu.pdf, accessed October 4, 2006.

5. Pucher, J. and J.L. Renne. 2003. *Socioeconomics of Urban Travel: Evidence from the 2001 NHTS.* Transportation Quarterly57 (3).

6. Voorhees, 2003. *Pedestrian Friendliness Scorecard.* Transportation Policy Institute. Retrieved March 1, 2006, from http://activelivingresearch.org/index.php/Tools_and_Measures/312

7. Berube, A., E. Deaken, and S. Raphael, 2006. *Socioeconomic Differences in Household Automobile Ownership Rates: Implications for Evacuation Policy.* Retrieved July 12, 2007, from http://socrates/berkeley.edu/~raphael/BerubeDeakenRaphael.pdf

8. Stutts, J.C. and W.W. Hunter, 1997. *Injuries to Pedestrians and Bicyclists: An Analysis Based on Hospital Emergency Department Data,* Publication No. FHWA-RD-99-078. Federal Highway Administration, US DOT, Washington DC.

9. Hunter, W.H., J.C. Stutts, and W.E. Pein, 1995. *Pedestrian Crash Types: A 1990's Informational Guide,* Publication No. FHWA-RD-96-163. Federal Highway Administration, US DOT, Washington DC.

10. Harkey, D.L. and C.V. Zegeer, 2004. *PEDSAFE: Pedestrian Safety Guide and Countermeasure Selection System,* Publication No. FHWA-SA-04-003. Federal Highway Administration, US DOT, Washington DC.

11. UK Department of Transpostation, 1987. *Killing Speed & Saving Lives,* London, England.

12. American Association of State Highway and Transportation Officials (AASHTO), 2002. *Roadside Design Guide.,* Washington, DC.

13. Federal Highway Administration (FHWA), 2003. *Manual on Uniform Traffic Control Devices,* Federal Highway Administration, US DOT, Washington DC.

14. Federal Highway Administration (FHWA), 1999. *Designing Sidewalks and Trails for Access – Part 1 of 2 – Review of Existing Guides and Practices,* Washington, DC.

Master Prompt List

RSA Matrix

Universal Considerations (For Entire RSA Site)

I. Needs of Pedestrians: Do pedestrian facilities address the needs of all pedestrians?

II. Connectivity and Convenience of Pedestrian Facilities: Are safe, continuous, and convenient paths provided along pedestrian routes throughout the study area?

III. Traffic: Are design, posted, and operating traffic speeds compatible with pedestrian safety?

IV. Behavior: Do pedestrians or motorists regularly misuse or ignore pedestrian facilities?

V. Construction: Have the effects of construction on all pedestrians been addressed adequately?

VI. School Presence: Is the safety of children in school zones adequately considered?

Topic	Subtopic	RSA Zones			
		A. Streets	**B. Street Crossings**	**C. Parking Areas/Adjacent Developments**	**D. Transit Areas**
Pedestrian Facilities	1. Presence, Design, and Placement	Sidewalks, paths, ramps, and buffers	Crossing treatments, intersections	Sidewalks and paths	Seating, shelter, waiting/loading/unloading areas
	2. Quality, Condition, and Obstructions	Sidewalks, paths, ramps, and buffers	Crossing treatments (see prompts in A)	Sidewalks and paths (see prompts in A)	Seating, shelter, waiting/loading/unloading areas (see prompts in A)
	3. Continuity and Connectivity	Continuity/Connectivity with other streets and crossings	Continuity/connectivity of crossing to ped network; channelization of peds to appropriate crossing points	Continuity/connectivity of pedestrian facilities through parking lots/adjacent developments	Connectivity of ped network to transit stops
	4. Lighting	Pedestrian level lighting along the street	Lighting of crossing	Pedestrian level lighting in parking lots/adjacent developments (see prompts in A and B)	Lighting at and near transit stop
	5. Visibility	Visibility of all road users	Visibility of crossing/waiting pedestrians and oncoming traffic	Visibility of pedestrians and backing/turning vehicles; visibility of pedestrian path	Visibility of pedestrians/waiting passengers and vehicles/buses
Traffic	6. Access Management	Driveway placement and design along streets	Driveway placement next to intersections	Driveway placement and use in relation to pedestrian paths	n/a*
	7. Traffic Characteristics	Volume and speed of adjacent traffic, conflicting conditions	Volume and speed of traffic approaching crossing, conflicting movements	Traffic volume and speed in parking lots and developments, conflicting conditions	Volume and speed of adjacent traffic and traffic at crossings to bus stops, conflicting conditions
Traffic Control Devices	8. Signs and Pavement Markings	Use and condition of signs, pavement markings, and route indicators	Use and condition of signs, pavement markings, and crossing indicators	Use and condition of signs, pavement markings for travel path and crossing points	Use and condition of transit related signs and pavement markings
	9. Signals	n/a*	Presence, condition, timing, and phasing of signals	n/a*	See prompts in B

A. Streets

Master Prompt	Detailed Prompt		RSA Stages			
			planning	design	construction	post-construction
A.1 Presence, Design, and Placement	A.1.1	Are sidewalks provided along the street?	✔	✔	✔	✔
	A.1.2	If no sidewalk is present, is there a walkable shoulder (e.g. wide enough to accommodate cyclists/pedestrians) on the road or other pathway/trail nearby?	✔	✔	✔	✔
	A.1.3	Are shoulders/sidewalks provided on both sides of bridges?	✔	✔	✔	✔
	A.1.4	Is the sidewalk width adequate for pedestrian volumes?	✔	✔	✔	✔
	A.1.5	Is there adequate separation distance between vehicular traffic and pedestrians?	✔	✔	✔	✔
	A.1.6	Are sidewalk/street boundaries discernable to people with visual impairments?		✔	✔	✔
	A.1.7	Are ramps provided as an alternative to stairs?	✔	✔	✔	✔
A.2 Quality, Conditions, and Obstructions	A.2.1	Will snow storage disrupt pedestrian access or visibility?	✔	✔	✔	✔
	A.2.2	Is the path clear from both temporary and permanent obstructions?	✔	✔	✔	✔
	A.2.3	Is the walking surface too steep?	✔	✔	✔	✔
	A.2.4	Is the walking surface adequate and well-maintained?		✔	✔	✔
A.3 Continuity and Connectivity	A.3.1	Are sidewalks/walkable shoulders continuous and on both sides of the street?	✔	✔	✔	✔
	A.3.2	Are measures needed to direct pedestrians to safe crossing points and pedestrian access ways?		✔	✔	✔
A.4 Lighting	A.4.1	Is the sidewalk adequately lit?	✔	✔	✔	✔
	A.4.2	Does street lighting improve pedestrian visibility at night?	✔	✔	✔	✔
A.5 Visibility	A.5.1	Is the visibility of pedestrians walking along the sidewalk/shoulder adequate?	✔	✔	✔	✔
A.6 Driveways	A.6.1	Are the conditions at driveways intersecting sidewalks endangering pedestrians?		✔	✔	✔
	A.6.2	Does the number of driveways make the route undesirable for pedestrian travel?	✔	✔	✔	✔

A. Streets

Master Prompt	Detailed Prompt		RSA Stages			
			planning	design	construction	post-construction
A.7 Traffic Charachteristics	A.7.1	Are there any conflicts between bicycles and pedestrians on sidewalks?				✔
A.8 Signs and Pavement Markings	A.8.1	Are pedestrian travel zones clearly delineated from other modes of traffic through the use of striping, colored and/or textured pavement, signing, and other methods?		✔	✔	✔
	A.8.2	Is the visibility of signs and pavement markings adequate during the day and night?		✔	✔	✔

Appendix A: Prompt Lists

B. Street Crossings

Master Prompt	Detailed Prompt		RSA Stages			
			planning	design	construction	post-construction
B.1 Presence, Design, and Placement	B.1.1	Do wide curb radii lengthen pedestrian crossing distances and encourage high-speed right turns?		✔	✔	✔
	B.1.2	Do channelized right turn lanes minimize conflicts with pedestrians?		✔	✔	✔
	B.1.3	Does a skewed intersection direct drivers' focus away from crossing pedestrians?	✔	✔	✔	✔
	B.1.4	Are pedestrian crossings located in areas where sight distance may be a problem?	✔	✔	✔	✔
	B.1.5	Do raised medians provide a safe waiting area (refuge) for pedestrians?	✔	✔	✔	✔
	B.1.6	Are supervised crossings adequately staffed by qualified crossing guards?				✔
	B.1.7	Are marked crosswalks wide enough?		✔	✔	✔
	B.1.8	Do at-grade railroad crossings accommodate pedestrians safely?		✔	✔	✔
	B.1.9	Are crosswalks sited along pedestrian desire lines?	✔	✔	✔	✔
	B.1.10	Are corners and curb ramps appropriately planned and designed at each approach to the crossing?		✔	✔	✔
B.2 Quality, Condition, and Obstructions	See prompts in Section A for potential issues on obstructions and protruding objects that apply to street crossings					
	B.2.1	Is the crossing pavement adequate and well maintained?				✔
	B.2.2	Is the crossing pavement flush with the roadway surface?			✔	✔
B.3 Continuity and Connectivity	B.3.1	Does pedestrian network connectivity continue through crossings by means of adequate, waiting areas at corners, curb ramps and marked crosswalks?	✔	✔	✔	✔
	B.3.2	Are pedestrians clearly directed to crossing points and pedestrian access ways?		✔	✔	✔
B.4 Lighting	B.4.1	Is the pedestrian crossing adequately lit?	✔	✔	✔	✔

B. Street Crossings

Master Prompt	Detailed Prompt		RSA Stages			
			planning	design	construction	post-construction
B.5 Visibility	B.5.1	Can pedestrians see approaching vehicles at all legs of the intersection/crossing and vice versa?	✔	✔	✔	✔
	B.5.2	Is the distance from the stop (or yield) line to a crosswalk sufficient for drivers to see pedestrians?		✔	✔	✔
	B.5.3	Do other conditions exist where stopped vehicles may obstruct visibility of pedestrians?		✔	✔	✔
B.6 Access Management	B.6.1	Are driveways placed close to crossings?	✔	✔	✔	✔
B.7 Traffic Characteristics	B.7.1	Do turning vehicles pose a hazard to pedestrians?				✔
	B.7.2	Are there sufficient gaps in the traffic to allow pedestrians to cross the road?	✔	✔	✔	✔
	B.7.3	Do traffic operations (especially during peak periods) create a safety concern for pedestrains?				✔
B.8 Signs and Pavement Markings	B.8.1	Is paint on stop bars and crosswalks worn, or are signs worn, missing, or damaged?			✔	✔
	B.8.2	Are crossing points for pedestrians properly signed and/or marked?		✔	✔	✔
B.9 Signals	B.9.1	Are pedestrian signal heads provided and adequate?		✔	✔	✔
	B.9.2	Are traffic and pedestrian signals timed so that wait times and crossing times are reasonable?		✔	✔	✔
	B.9.3	Is there a problem because of an inconsistency in pedestrian actuation (or detection) types?	✔	✔	✔	✔
	B.9.4	Are all pedestrian signals and push buttons functioning correctly and safely?			✔	✔
	B.9.5	Are ADA accessible push buttons provided and properly located?		✔	✔	✔

C. Parking Areas/Adjacent Developments

Master Prompt	Detailed Prompt		RSA Stages			
			planning	design	construction	post-construction
C.1 Presence, Design, and Placement	C.1.1	Do sidewalks/paths connect the street and adjacent land uses?	✔	✔	✔	✔
	C.1.2	Are the sidewalks/paths designed appropriately?		✔	✔	✔
	C.1.3	Are buildings entrances located and designed to be obvious and easily accessible to pedestrians?	✔	✔	✔	✔
C.2 Quality, Condition, and Obstructions	See prompts in Section **A** for potential issues on obstructions and protruding opbjects that apply to sidewalks and walkways at parking areas/adjacent developments					
	See prompts in Section **A** for potential issues on surface conditions that apply to sidewalks and walkways at parking areas/adjacent developments					
	C.2.1	Do parked vehicles obstruct pedestrian paths?				✔
C.3 Continuity and Connectivity	C.3.1	Are pedestrian facilities continuous? Do they provide adequate connections for pedestrian traffic?	✔	✔	✔	✔
	C.3.2	Are transitions of pedestrian facilities between developments/projects adequate?		✔	✔	✔
C.4 Lighting	See prompts in Section **A and B** for potential issues on lighting that apply to sidewalks and walkways at parking areas/adjacent developments					
C.5 Visibility	C.5.1	Are visibility and sight distance adequate?	✔	✔	✔	✔
C.6 Access Management	C.6.1	Are travel paths for pedestrians and other vehicle modes clearly delineated at access openings?	✔	✔	✔	✔
	C.6.2	Do drivers look for and yield to pedestrian when turning into and out of driveways?			✔	✔
C.7 Traffic Characteristics	C.7.1	Does pedestrian or driver behavior increase the risk of a pedestrian collision?				✔
	C.7.2	Are buses, cars, bicycles, and pedestrians separated on the site and provided with their own designated areas for travel?	✔	✔	✔	✔
C.8 Signs and Pavement Markings	C.8.1	Are travel paths and crossing points for pedestrians properly signed and/or marked?		✔	✔	✔

D. Transit Areas

Master Prompt	Detailed Prompt		RSA Stages			
			planning	design	construction	post-construction
D.1 Presence, Design, and Placement	D.1.1	Are bus stops sited properly?	✔	✔	✔	✔
	D.1.2	Are safe pedestrian crossings convenient for transit and school bus users?	✔	✔	✔	✔
	D.1.3	Is sight distance to bus stops adequate?	✔	✔	✔	✔
	D.1.4	Are shelters appropriately designed and placed for pedestrian safety and convenience?		✔	✔	✔
D.2 Quality, Condition, and Obstructions	D.2.1	Is the seating area at a safe and comfortable distance from vehicle and bicycle lanes?		✔	✔	✔
	D.2.2	Do seats (or persons sitting on them) obstruct the sidewalk or reduce its usable width?		✔	✔	✔
	D.2.3	Is a sufficient landing area provided to accommodate waiting passengers, boarding/alighting passengers, and through/bypassing pedestrian traffic at peak times?		✔	✔	✔
	D.2.4	Is the landing area paved and free of problems such as uneven surfaces, standing water, or steep slopes?		✔	✔	✔
	D.2.5	Is the sidewalk free of temporary/permanent obstructions that constrict its width or block access to the bus stop?	✔	✔	✔	✔
D.3 Continuity and Connectivity	D.3.1	Is the nearest crossing opportunity free of potential hazards for pedestrians?	✔	✔	✔	✔
	D.3.2	Are transit stops part of a continuous network of pedestrian facilities?	✔	✔	✔	✔
	D.3.3	Are transit stops maintained during periods of inclement weather?		✔	✔	✔
D.4 Lighting	D.4.1	Are access ways to transit facilities well-lit to accommodate early-morning, late-afternoon, and evening	✔	✔	✔	✔
D.5 Visibility	D.5.1	Are open sight lines maintained between approaching buses and passenger waiting and loading areas?		✔	✔	✔
D.7 Traffic Characteristics	D.7.1	Do pedestrians entering and leaving buses conflict with cars, bicycles, or other pedestrians?		✔	✔	✔
D.8 Signs and Pavement Markings	D.8.1	Are appropriate signs and pavement markings provided for school bus and transit stops?		✔	✔	✔

BIBLIOGRAPHY OF PEDESTRIAN ROAD SAFETY AUDIT AND ASSESSMENT RESOURCES

This bibliography contains information about the known available resources for conducting pedestrian oriented RSAs and assessments. Except where noted, these resources are intended to be used by professionals with adequate experience in road safety practices and principles, as well as some experience in pedestrian safety. The RSA team will probably be familiar with the general references; however, the references for pedestrian specific RSAs may not be familiar to RSA team members.

General Road Safety Audit Resources

Table 1 presents general RSA resources. These guides provide detailed information about the RSA process and are critical to helping engineers understand the objectives of an RSA and training auditors to examine safety from the perspective of all road users, including pedestrians.

TABLE 1: GENERAL ROAD SAFETY AUDIT RESOURCES

Name and Characteristics	Source	Topic Areas
Name: **Road Safety Audits, NCHRP Synthesis 336** *Purpose*: To examine the state of the practice of road safety audit review applications for U.S. states and Canadian provinces. This synthesis also reviews international RSA practices. *Number of questions*: ~500, many repeated *Assessment Area*: all areas *Manual included*: no *Scoring mechanism*: no	Wilson, Eugene, and Martin Lipinski, *Road Safety Audits*, NCHRP Synthesis 336, Transportation Research Board, Washington D.C., 2004.	• Drainage • Climate conditions • Landscaping • Roadway cross section • Lighting • Signage • Delineation • Pavement markings • Roadway surface
Name: **Road Safety Audit 2nd Edition** *Purpose*: Draw together current practices in Australia, New Zealand, and elsewhere to provide practitioners and decision makers in State highway authorities, local government authorities, and consulting practices of formally addressing road safety issues. *Number of questions*: 800 (75 ped oriented) *Assessment area*: All areas *Manual included*: no *Scoring mechanism*: no	Austroads	• General Topic • Design Issues • Alignment Details • Intersections • Special Road Users • Signs • Lighting • Delineation • Pavement Markings • Physical Objects • Operations • Traffic Management • Traffic Signals • Parking • Bridges • Etc.

TABLE 1: GENERAL ROAD SAFETY AUDIT RESOURCES

Name and Characteristics	Source	Topic Areas
Name: **Road Safety Audit Guidelines** *Purpose*: Provide transportation agencies and independent auditors with a sequence of techniques and instructions for the undertaking of a road safety audit. The document is a composite of current practices from various jurisdictions tailored to Canadian roads, design practices, and operating conditions. *Number of questions*: 315 (37 ped oriented) *Assessment area*: All areas *Manual included*: no *Scoring mechanism*: no	University of New Brunswick Transportation Group Department of Civil Engineering Fredericton, New Brunswick Sponsored by: Maritime Road Development Corporation National Research Council's Industrial Research Assistance Program	• General Observations • Alignment and Cross Sections • Intersections • Road Surface • Visual Aids • Physical Objects • Road Users • Access and Adjacent Development • Parking
Name: **Road Safety Audit Guidelines** *Purpose*: To provide guidance for performing road safety audits. *Number of questions*: N/A *Assessment area*: All areas *Manual included*: no *Scoring mechanism*: no	Federal Highway Administration Report FHWA-SA-06-06 by: J. McGill; B. Malone; O. Tonkonjenkov; J. Suggett; B. Wemple; and J. Freeman	• Road Safety Audits • Road Design • Risk Assessment • Transportation Planning

General Pedestrian RSAs

The RSA resources in Table 2 were generally developed for assessing existing facilities (as opposed to design plans or pre-construction facilities). The resources can be divided into two major groups based on the purpose of the assessment: the ability of the audit to assess the pedestrian environment in terms of 1) its impact on the safety of its users, or 2) its impact on "walkability" or the promotion of physical activity. Some of the materials were developed for use by a trained or expert RSA team, while others were less formal and were developed more for community members to be able to assess their neighborhood conditions.

TABLE 2: GENERAL PEDESTRIAN ASSESSMENTS

Name and Characteristics	Source	Topic Areas
Name: **Systematic Pedestrian and Cycling Environmental Scan (SPACES)** *Purpose*: Measure physical environmental factors that may have an effect on walking and cycling behaviors in local neighborhoods (i.e., for health promotion) *Number of questions*: 37 *Assessment area*: street segments only; local residential areas *Manual included*: yes; 28 page user guide *Scoring mechanism*: no	University of Western Australia; Described in: Pikora, T., Bull, F., Jamrozik, K. et al., "Developing a Reliable Audit Instrument to Measure the Physical Environment For Physical Activity," *American Journal of Preventative Medicine*, 23(3), 2002, 187-194. Available online from Active Living By Design web site http://www.activelivingresearch.org/ index.php/SPACES_instrument/323	• Measures Of Function (E.G. Walking/Cycling Surface, Streets, And Traffic) • Safety (Personal And Traffic) • Aesthetics (Streetscape and Views) • Destinations • Subjective Assessment
Name: **Sidewalk Assessment Tool** *Purpose*: Assess the maintenance of sidewalks; provide index score for comparing different sidewalk conditions *Number of questions*: 5 *Assessment area*: sidewalk segment *Manual included*: no *Scoring mechanism*: from 1 to 3 for each variable	Williams J.E., M. Evans, K.A. Kirtland, M.M. Cavnar, P.A. Sharpe, M.J. Neet, and A. Cook, *Sidewalk Assessment Tool*, Prevention Research Center, Arnold School of Public Health, University of South Carolina.	• Levelness • Artificial Items Blocking the Path • Natural Items Blocking the Path • Cleanliness • Surface Condition
Name: **Pedestrian Safety and Accessibility Audit Checklist** *Purpose*: Identify inadequate or unsafe pedestrian facilities; to improve pedestrian safety, accessibility, and amenity (i.e., for safety) *Number of questions*: 105 *Assessment area*: sidewalk segment *Manual included*: no *Scoring mechanism*: no	"3.11: Pedestrian Safety and Accessibility Audit Tools," Traffic and Road Use Management Manual, Volume 3, Queensland Government, Department of Main Roads, March 24, 2005, available online at http://www.mainroads.qld.gov.au/MRWEB/Prod/Content.nsf/	• Land Use and Context • Footpaths/Sidewalks • Ped Facilities and Accessibility • Catering For Ped Groups • Traffic Volumes • Schools • Traffic and Road Environment • Temporary Roadworks • Signing/Marking • Lighting • Visibility • Fencing • Amenities

Appendix B: Supplemental Information

TABLE 2: GENERAL PEDESTRIAN ASSESSMENTS

Name and Characteristics	Source	Topic Areas
Name: **ACES Community Assessment** *Purpose*: Assess the health of a community and identify ways to increase opportunities for physical activity in the community (i.e., for health promotion) *Number of questions*: 68 *Assessment area*: Pedestrian roadway environments *Manual included*: no *Scoring mechanism*: point structure for each question to calculate a total score to be compared against 5 different levels of excellence	"Creating Active Community Environments (ACEs): Community Assessment," Eat Smart, Move More… North Carolina Web Site, NC Department of Health and Human Services, NC Division of Public Health, (no date), available online at http://www. eatsmartmovemorenc. com/programs/aces/aces_ commassess.pdf.	• Policies and Planning for Nonmotorized Transportation • Pedestrian and Bicycle Safety and Procedures • Community Resources for Physical Activity • Schools • Public Transportation
Name: **PEDS Audit Protocol** *Purpose*: Measure physical environmental factors that may have an effect on walking behaviors in local neighborhoods (i.e., for health promotion) *Number of questions*: 35 *Assessment area*: Community-wide walking environment *Manual included*: yes *Scoring mechanism*: no	Clifton, Kelly J., Andrea Livi, and Daniel Rodriguez, *The Development and Testing of an Audit for the Pedestrian Environment*, Draft, no date.	• Environment • Pedestrian Facilities • Road Attributes • Walking/Cycling Environment • Subjective Assessment
Name: **Walking Suitability Assessment** *Purpose*: Assess the suitability of sidewalks for walking and roads for bicycling (i.e., for health promotion) *Number of questions*: 15 *Assessment area*: sidewalk/path *Manual included*: no *Scoring mechanism*: Up to 7-point Likert scale to calculate a final suitability score	Emery, J.E., C.E. Crump, and P. Bors, "Reliability and Validity of Two Instruments Designed to Assess the Walking and Bicycling Suitability of Sidewalks and Roads." *American Journal of Health Promotion*, September/ October 2003, 18 (1), pp. 38-46.	• Sidewalk Presence, Condition, Width, & Material • Ramp • Lighting • AADT • Motor Vehicle Speed • Buffer Width • Number of Traffic Lanes
Name: **Safety Audit Checklist for Dual Use Paths** *Purpose*: Assess the crash potential and safety performance of the road or road proposal (i.e., for safety) *Number of questions*: 70 *Assessment area*: walking conditions on both sides of the street *Manual included*: yes *Scoring mechanism*: no	Main Roads, *Safety Audit Checklist for Dual Use Paths*, Western Australia, September 1997.	• General Items • Alignment and Cross Section • Intersections • Signs • Lighting • Traffic Signals • Physical Objects • Pavements

TABLE 2: GENERAL PEDESTRIAN ASSESSMENTS

Name and Characteristics	Source	Topic Areas
Name: **PEDSAFE Pedestrian Audit** *Purpose*: To evaluate the general quality and safety of the pedestrian environment (i.e., for safety) *Number of questions*: 45 *Assessment area*: Roadway as it relates to pedestrians *Manual included*: no *Scoring mechanism*: no	Lillis, J., and S. Pourmoradian, *PEDSAFE Pedestrian Audit*, 2001. Available online at www.pedbiketrans.asn.au/rframset.html	• Levels of Connectivity • Pedestrian Volumes • Vehicle Traffic and Speed • Form of Corridor • Street Crossings • Footpaths • Street Furniture • Signs • Special Needs Groups • General Amenity
Name: **Street Observation Response Sheet** *Purpose*: To survey the heart healthy environmental supports of a community (i.e., for health promotion) *Number of questions*: 40 *Assessment area*: Roadway corridor as it relates to pedestrians *Manual included*: no *Scoring mechanism*: no	Eisenberg, Bonnie, *Street Observation Response Sheet*, Draft, New York State Department of Health, Heart Healthy Program, 2003. Contact info: Bonnie Eisenberg, NYS DOH, (518) (473-0673).	• Sidewalk Observations • Street Crossing Observations • Street Observations • General Environment and Amenities
Name: **Walkability Index** *Purpose*: To determine the "walkability" or foot-friendliness of a neighborhood *Number of questions*: 10 *Assessment area*: Pedestrian environment at the census block *Manual included*: no *Scoring mechanism*: Provides points for each question; final score produces index between 0.45 and 2.0	Bradshaw, C., *Creating and Using a Rating System for Neighborhood Walkability*, Presented to the 14th International Pedestrian Conference, Boulder, CO, October 1993.	• Density • Parking • Number of Sitting Spots • Destinations • Parkland • Sidewalks
Name: **Footpaths, Walkways, and Cyclepaths Checklist** *Purpose*: To assess the quality of footpaths, walkways, and cyclepaths in a community (i.e. to promote public health) *Number of questions*: 89 *Assessment area*: Pedestrian environment in the neighborhood *Manual included*: no *Scoring mechanism*: no	New South Wales Health & Centre for Population Health, *Footpath, Walkway, and Cyclepath Checklist*, September 1997.	• Curbs And Ramps • Steps/Stairs/Ramps • Driveways • Width of Footpaths • Obstructions • Covers and Gratings • Setbacks • Gradients • Surface Treatments • Personal Safety

TABLE 2: GENERAL PEDESTRIAN ASSESSMENTS

Name and Characteristics	Source	Topic Areas
Name: **Neighborhood Walking Audit** *Purpose*: To determine the "walkability" of an area *Number of questions*: 13 *Assessment area*: Pedestrian facilities in neighborhoods *Manual included*: no *Scoring mechanism*: Users rank overall sections on scale of 1 to 5	Ross, Author, *Neighborhood Walking and Bicycling Audits*, City of Madison, Department of Transportation, Madison, WI, no date.	• Sidewalk Facilities • Street Crossings • Traffic Signals • Convenience • Enjoyability • Etc.
Name: **Walkability Audit Form** *Purpose*: To determine the "walkability" of an area *Number of questions*: 29 *Assessment area*: Pedestrian environment *Manual included*: no *Scoring mechanism*: no	United Seniors of Oakland and Alameda County, *Walkability Audit Form*, available online at http://www.transcoalition.org/ia/pedinfra/14.html.	• Sidewalks • Street Crossings • Traffic and Drivers • Visibility and Signage • Desirability/Appeal of the Area
Name: **Community Assessment Tool** *Purpose*: To determine the "walkability" of an area *Number of questions*: 110 *Assessment area*: Pedestrian environment *Manual included*: no *Scoring mechanism*: no	National Center for Bicycling and Walking, *Community Assessment Tool*, December 2002, available online at http://www.bikewalk.org/vision/community_assessment.htm.	• Transportation • Land Use and Development • Schools • Parks, Recreation, and Trails • Safety, Security, and Crime Prevention
Name: **Walking and Bicycling Indicators** *Purpose*: To determine the "walkability" of an area *Number of questions*: 30 *Assessment area*: Pedestrian environment *Manual included*: no *Scoring mechanism*: no	National Center for Bicycling and Walking, *Walking and Bicycling Indicators*, no date, available online at http://www.bikewalk.org/vision/community_assessment.htm.	• Transportation • Land Use and Development • Schools • Parks, Recreation, and Trails • Safety, Security, and Crime Prevention
Name: **PBIC Walkability Checklist** *Purpose*: To determine the "walkability" of an area *Number of questions*: 5 *Assessment area*: Pedestrian environment *Manual included*: no *Scoring mechanism*: Rate responses on a scale of 1 to 6 and compare to given total scale	Pedestrian and Bicycle Information Center, *Walkability Checklist*, US Department of Transportation, available online at http://www.walkinginfo.org/walkingchecklist.htm.	• Sidewalk Facilities • Ease of Crossings • Driver Behavior • Safety Rules • Pleasantness of Walk

TABLE 2: GENERAL PEDESTRIAN ASSESSMENTS

Name and Characteristics	Source	Topic Areas
Name: **Handout 16: Walkability Checklist** *Purpose*: To determine the "walkability" of an area *Number of questions*: 43 *Assessment area*: Pedestrian environment *Manual included*: no *Scoring mechanism*: Rate overall sections on a scale of 1 to 5 and compare to given total scale	Active Independent Aging, *Handout 16: Walkability Checklist*, University of Ottawa and the Public Health and Long Term Care Branch, City of Ottawa, available online at http://www.falls-chutes.com/guide/english/resources/handouts/pdf/WalkabilityChecklist.pdf	• Sidewalks, Stairs and Ramps, Winter Safety • Crosswalks • Traffic • Personal Safety • Walking Routes
Name: **Walkability Audit Tool** *Purpose*: Assess the walkability surrounding a workplace *Number of questions*: 9 *Assessment area*: Pedestrian environment around workplace *Manual included*: no *Scoring mechanism*: Weighted scoring for all 9 categories for a total score out of 100 possible points	Centers for Disease Control, *Worksite Walkability: Audit Tool*, available online at http://www.cdc.gov/nccdphp/dnpa/walkability/audit_tool.htm.	• Pedestrian Facilities • Pedestrian Conflicts • Crosswalks • Maintenance • Path Size • Buffer • Accessibility • Aesthetics • Shade
Name: **Community Street Audit** *Purpose*: To determine the "walkability" of an area *Number of questions*: 9 *Assessment area*: Pedestrian environment *Manual included*: no *Scoring mechanism*: no	Living Streets Aotearoa Inc, Community Street Audit, available online at http://www.livingstreets.org.nz/pdf/DIY_Street_Audit.pdf.	• Footway Surfaces and Obstructions • Facilities • Signage • Maintenance and Enforcement • Personal Security • Crossings • Roadway Design • Aesthetics • Traffic • Economic Environment
Name: **The Irvine Minnesota Inventory** *Purpose*: To measure a wide range of built environment features that are potentially linked to active living, especially walking *Number of questions*: 160 *Assessment area*: Pedestrian environment *Manual included*: yes *Scoring mechanism*: some questions contain rating scale from 0 to 3; others are yes/no	Day, K., Boarnet, M., Alfonzo, M. & Forsyth, A. (2006). The Irvine-Minnesota Inventory to measure built environments: Development. *American Journal of Preventive Medicine*, 30(2), 144-152. Available online at: http://webfiles.uci.edu/kday/public/index.html	• Accessibility • Pleasurability • Perceived Safety from Traffic • Perceived Safety from Crime

TABLE 2: GENERAL PEDESTRIAN ASSESSMENTS

Name and Characteristics	Source	Topic Areas
Name: **Creating Walkable Communities: A Walkable Guide for Local Governments** *Purpose*: The document is intended to serve as a tool for local governments and concerned citizens for guidelines, suggestions, and techniques on how to make communities more walkable and pedestrian friendly. *Number of questions*: 275 *Assessment area*: All areas *Manual included*: no *Scoring mechanism*: no	Bicycle Federation of America Campaign to Make America Walkable	• Design • Sidewalks • ADA • Driveways • Crosswalks • Medians • Parking • Landscaping • Lighting, Signs • Traffic Calming • Bridges • Commercial and Residential Zoning
Name: **City of Phoenix 2005 Pedestrian Safety Audit** *Purpose*: Improve pedestrian safety through a periodic review of areas with a high pedestrian crash experience. *Number of questions*: 15 *Assessment area*: All areas *Manual included*: no *Scoring mechanism*: no	City of Phoenix Street Transportation Department	• Ramps • Pavement Markings • Pedestrian Signals • Warning Signs
Name: **Walkable Places Survey** *Purpose*: To measure barriers to improve walkability *Number of questions*: no details provided *Assessment area*: Pedestrian environment in neighborhood *Manual included*: no *Scoring mechanism*: no	Shriver, Katherine, *Walkable Places Survey*, The Walkable Places Project, 2002, available online at http://www.walkableplaces.com/audits1.htm	• No Details Provided
Name: **Pedestrian Policies and Design Guideline 2005** *Purpose*: To assess the extent to which an area is safe, comfortable or a destination. *Number of questions*: 88 *Assessment area*: All areas *Manual included*: no *Scoring mechanism*: Each question has a rating scale from 1 to 5	Maricopa Association of Governments, available online at http://www.mag.maricopa.gov/detail.cms?item=4906	• Sidewalks • Crosswalks • Signal Timing • Access • Pedestrian Environment • Pedestrian Amenities • Driver Behavior • Transit / Bus • School Zones

RSAs in School Zones

The resources in the Table 3 focus on assessing existing facilities in school zones. The purpose of auditing the school area is to: 1) assess the safety for school children who walk to school, or 2) assess the school route's "walkability" to assist in the promotion of physical activity. Most of the materials were developed for use by a trained RSA team.

TABLE 3: SCHOOL ASSESSMENTS

Name and Characteristics	Source	Topic Areas
Name: **Safe Routes to School Checklist** *Purpose:* Examine the school route (for safety) *Number of questions:* 11 *Assessment area:* School Route *Manual included:* No *Scoring mechanism:* No	Roosevelt Elementary, Santa Barbara, CA	• Presence of Sidewalk/Path • Obstacles • # of Street Crossings • Driver Characteristics • Purpose for Choosing Mode and Preferences • School Drop Off Zone
Name: **School Site Assessment for Traffic Safety** *Purpose:* Examine biking and walking conditions at the school (for safety) *Number of questions:* 73 *Assessment area:* School site *Manual included:* No *Scoring mechanism:* No	Florida Traffic and Bicycle Safety Education Program	• Administration and Policy • School Traffic Safety Teams • Student Travel Patterns • School Traffic Design at the School Site Regarding Drop Off Areas, Walkways, Crossings, Etc. • Safety Education Programs Including Crossing Guards, Safety Patrols, and Traffic Education
Name: **Neighborhood Site Assessment** *Purpose:* Examine biking and walking conditions on the route to school (for safety) *Number of questions:* 4 *Assessment area:* School route *Manual included:* Provides instructions and description of conditions to consider *Scoring mechanism:* No	Florida Traffic and Bicycle Safety Education Program	• Major Streets and Transportation Facilities • Street Crossings • Sidewalks • Safety/Security Concerns
Name: **Protocol for Walkability** *Purpose:* Environmental assessment to determine how walkable schools are (for health) *Number of questions:* 48 *Assessment area:* School route *Manual included:* Provides 14 page Home to School Observational Coding *Scoring mechanism:* No	St. Louis University; Dr. Matthew Kreuter	• Sidewalks • Street Crossings • Driver Behavior • Safety • Visual Appeal

TABLE 3: SCHOOL ASSESSMENTS

Name and Characteristics	Source	Topic Areas
Name: **School Crossing Safety Audit Form** *Purpose:* Examine biking and walking conditions on the route to school (for safety) *Number of questions:* 21 *Assessment area:* School route *Manual included:* Provides 7-page *School Crossing Safety Audit Procedure* for assisting in performing the audit *Scoring mechanism:* Provides point system for each question; 148 points possible (higher is worse) on first 19 questions; additional points for crash history	City of Phoenix Street Transportation Department	• Student Characteristics • Presence of Sidewalks And Other Pedestrian Facilities • Traffic Conditions • Crossing Characteristics (Location, Control, Visibility, Etc.) • Waiting Areas • Presence of Supervision • Crash Records
Name: **School Crossing Review** *Purpose:* Examine safety of roadway crossings on the route to school *Number of questions:* 3 *Assessment area:* Intersections *Manual included:* No *Scoring mechanism:* No	City of Phoenix Street Transportation Department	• Number of Student Crossings • Unusual Traffic Conditions • Unusual Student Conditions
Name: **Gregory Heights SW2S** *Purpose:* Simplify the national SRTS materials; student activity for 6 and 7 grade class(es); one question for parents *Number of questions:* 10 *Assessment area:* Trip to School *Manual included:* No *Scoring mechanism:* Simple multiple choice	Jere Fitterman via email to Nancy Pullen	• Grade and Gender • Distance of Trip • Usual Modes and Reasons for Mode Choice • Behavioral/Attitudinal Questions on Perceived Safety • Parents: Changes Before Allow Children to Walk/Bike to School
Name: **California Walk to School Day Walkability Checklist** *Purpose:* Promote W2S, identify barriers, collect behavioral data *Number of questions:* 9 *Assessment area:* Trip to School *Manual included:* No *Scoring mechanism:* Simple multiple choice	California Walk to School HQ www.cawalktoschool.com	• General Infrastructure • Driver Behavior at Drop-Off Zone • Positive Factors • Mode Preference • Barriers • Zip Code
Name: **Lexington Fayette Pedestrian Facility Inventory** *Purpose:* Broad inventory existing conditions *Number of questions:* ~35 plus intersection diagram *Assessment area:* Intersection or street *Manual included:* No; definitions of data codes *Scoring mechanism:* Checkboxes for presence; fill in dimensions	Kenzie Gleason, Bike-Ped Coordinator, LFUCG	• Crosswalk and Sidewalk Facilities • Signage • Street Characteristics • Amenities; Incl. Dimensions

TABLE 3: SCHOOL ASSESSMENTS

Name and Characteristics	Source	Topic Areas
Name: **Maryland Safe Routes to School Audit** *Purpose:* Broad assessment of infrastructure, operations, attitudes *Number of questions:* 43 *Assessment area:* School site with adjacent crossings *Manual included:* Yes for Neighborhood Site Audit (see Part 2) *Scoring mechanism:* Combination checkboxes, multiple choice, open ended, diagrams	State of Maryland Council on Physical Fitness (on-line)	• Drop Off Area: Signage, Student and Driver Behavior; Loading Zone Characteristics • Sidewalks and Bike Routes: Separation From Traffic, Rams, Lighting, Regularly Used • Adjacent Intersections: Traffic Volumes, Controls, Signals; Sight Distances • Signs • Signals.
Name: **Maryland Safe Routes to School Audit** *Purpose:* Broad assessment of infrastructure, operations, attitudes *Number of questions:* 50 *Assessment area:* Neighborhood site audit *Manual included:* Yes *Scoring mechanism:* Combination checkboxes, multiple choice, open ended, diagrams	State of Maryland Council on Physical Fitness (on-line)	• Crosswalks: Signals, Driver Behavior, Medians, Traffic Calming Facilities, ADT Counts, Sketch of Intersection • Road Segment: Driveways • Driver Behavior • Known Crash History • Sidewalk Facilities • Grades • Buffers • Security • Dogs • Crime • Loitering • Fights.
Name: **Maryland Safe Routes to School Audit** *Purpose:* Broad assessment of infrastructure, operations, attitudes *Number of questions:* 42 *Assessment area:* Parent survey *Manual included:* Yes for Neighborhood Site Audit (see Part 2) *Scoring mechanism:* Combination checkboxes, multiple choice, open ended, diagrams	State of Maryland Council on Physical Fitness (on-line)	• Child Data • Distance of Trip, Route • Likert Scale on Conditions • Influences on Decision to Allow Oldest Child to Walk to School • Factors that Should Change • Education Outreach Programs Interested in Learning More About

Appendix B: Supplemental Information

TABLE 3: SCHOOL ASSESSMENTS

Name and Characteristics	Source	Topic Areas
Name: **Pennsylvania KHR (Keystone Healthy Routes)** *Purpose:* Basis for planning a KHR program *Number of questions:* 35 plus school site map and traffic count *Assessment area:* School site *Manual included:* Cover sheet and for each subsection *Scoring mechanism:* Diagram school site; yes/no plus open ended elaboration questions	Keystone Healthy Routes website	• Lower Proportion of Infrastructure Questions, Focus on Policy, Education, Behavior.

Transit Assessments

Most of the transit assessment materials focus on assessing the environment around bus stations (with the exception of the *Inventory of Pedestrian Facilities around Transit*, which includes rail stops). All of the materials in Table 4 focus on assessing existing facilities.

TABLE 4: TRANSIT ASSESSMENTS

Name and Characteristics	Source	Topic Areas
Name: **Bus Stop Assessment Sheet** *Purpose:* Evaluate pedestrian access features and connections; assess passenger comfort amenities; evaluate safety and security features; document information features *Number of questions:* 42 *Assessment area:* Bus stops and surrounding areas *Manual included:* no *Scoring mechanism:* no	Ramond Robinson, Triangle Transit Authority	• Size, Location, and Material of Landing Area • Sidewalk Width and Connectivity • Shelter Attributes • Seating Adequacy • Speed Limit • Traffic • Parking • Lighting • Signage
Name: **Arlington Bus Stop Assessment** *Purpose:* Describe location, surroundings landing area, connections, amenities, seating, safety, information *Number of questions:* 86 *Assessment area:* Bus stops and surrounding areas *Manual included:* no *Scoring mechanism:* no	NCTR report – *Safer Stops for Vulnerable Customers* (Tucker, 2003)	• Adjacent Properties • Landing Area Size • Location and Material • Trip Generators • Sidewalk Width and Connectivity • Shelter Attributes • Seating; Trash; Newspaper Boxes • Speed Limit • Parking • Travel Lanes • Lighting • Pay Phones • Landscaping • Information

TABLE 4: TRANSIT ASSESSMENTS

Name and Characteristics	Source	Topic Areas
Name: **Inventory of Pedestrian Facilities around Transit** *Purpose*: Perform inventory around transit stations for MARTA, CCT, C-Tran and Gwinnett *Number of questions*: 24 *Assessment area*: Bus stops and surrounding areas (half-mile radius) *Manual included*: no *Scoring mechanism*: no	Atlanta Regional Commission http://www.atlantaregional.com/transportationair/InventSurvey.pdf	• Land Uses • Sidewalk Characteristics • Pedestrian Crossing Features
Name: **Technical Guidelines for the Placement of Transit Stops** *Purpose*: Assist in siting transit stops for operations and safety *Number of questions*: 0 *Assessment area*: n/a *Manual included*: n/a *Scoring mechanism*: n/a	Toronto Transit Commission Service Planning Department, May 2004	• Stop Spacing • Selecting the Best Location for a Stop • Site-Specific Considerations • Stop Markers • Shelters
Name: **Local Bus Checklist** *Purpose*: Evaluate safety and convenience issues at bus stops *Number of questions*: 13 *Assessment area*: Bus stops and surrounding areas *Manual included*: no *Scoring mechanism*: no	Alameda Transit Advocates, Alameda, CA Contact: Susan Decker, decker@avax.net	• Presence or Absence of Map • Schedule • Shelter • Bench • Trash Receptacle • Sidewalk Width • Curb Condition • Sidewalk Condition • Pedestrian Access to Stop • Quality of Transit Information • Surrounding Land Uses • Lighting • Sight Lines

Accessibility Assessments

The resources in Table 5 focus on access to facilities for various pedestrians (older pedestrians, pedestrians who are blind, pedestrians who use wheelchairs, etc.).

TABLE 5: ACCESSIBILITY ASSESSMENTS

Name and Characteristics	Source	Topic Areas
Name: **Accessible Sidewalks and Street Crossings – An Informational Guide** *Purpose*: A concise, informal, and illustrated booklet of ADA. *Number of questions*: 13 *Assessment area*: Accessible environment *Manual included*: yes *Scoring mechanism*: no	Federal Highway Administration (FHWA-SA-03-019)	• Sidewalks • Curb Ramps • Driveway Crossings • Median Cut-Throughs • Median Ramps • Protruding Objects • Grades • Etc.
Name: **PENNDOT Bicycle/Pedestrian Facilities Checklist** *Purpose*: Assess the design of a sports facility *Number of questions*: 29 *Assessment area*: Pedestrian environment *Manual included*: no *Scoring mechanism*: no	Pedestrian and Bicycle Coalition of Greater Philadelphia http://www.bicyclecoalition.org/presentations/padotchecklist.htm	• Curb Cuts • Slopes • Signals • Signage • Lighting • Etc.
Name: **Kentucky Government ADA Checklist** *Purpose*: Identify architectural and communication barriers encountered by people with disabilities, assist in planning for removal of barriers. *Number of questions*: 23 *Assessment area*: Bus facilities *Manual included*: no *Scoring mechanism*: no	Kentucky Department of Vocational Rehabilitation http://ada.ky.gov/documents/Checklist_2000.pdf	• Size of Sidewalks • Location of Signs • Handrails • Slopes and Cross-Slopes • Landings • Gratings • Etc.
Name: **ADA Checklist for New Lodging Facilities** *Purpose*: Help owners and managers of lodging facilities identify ADA mistakes. *Number of questions*: 20 *Assessment area*: Lodging facilities *Manual included*: no *Scoring mechanism*: no	U.S. Department of Justice Civil Rights Division Disability Rights Section http://www.ada.ufl.edu/ADAcd/cdpages/PDF_PUBS/HOTELCK/HSURVEY.PDF	• Size of Sidewalks • Ramps • Curb Cuts • Free of Barriers • Etc.
Name: **Public Rights of Way Design Guide, Checklist for Accessible Sidewalks and Street Crossings** *Purpose*: Provide standards for accessible rights of way *Number of questions*: 0 *Assessment area*: Pedestrian environment *Manual included*: no *Scoring mechanism*: no	U.S. Access Board and Federal Highway Administration http://www.access-board.gov/prowac/guide/PROWGuide.htm	• Ramps • Sidewalk Widths • Intersections • Lighting • Height of Signs • Drinking Fountains • Etc.

TABLE 5: ACCESSIBILITY ASSESSMENTS

Name and Characteristics	Source	Topic Areas
Name: **Survey Form 4: Ramps** *Purpose*: Assess ramp safety *Number of questions*: 21 *Assessment area*: Access ramps *Manual included*: no *Scoring mechanism*: no	U.S. Access Board http://www.access-board.gov/adaag/checklist/CurbRamps.html	• Slope • Visual Contrast • Textural Contrast • Transition • Visibility • Counter-Slope • Etc.
Name: **Survey Form 29A: Transportation Facilities – Bus Stops** *Purpose*: Assess accessibility to bus stops, stations, terminals, etc. *Number of questions*: 9 *Assessment area*: Bus stops *Manual included*: no *Scoring mechanism*: no	U.S. Access Board http://www.access-board.gov/ada-aba/checklist/TransportationBus.html	• Signage • Shelters • Connection to Ped ROW • Clear Dimensions • Etc.
Name: **Survey Form 3: Accessible Exterior Routes** *Purpose*: Assess accessibility of exterior routes *Number of questions*: 25 *Assessment area*: Pedestrian environment *Manual included*: no *Scoring mechanism*: no	U.S. Access Board http://www.access-board.gov/ada-aba/checklist/ExteriorAccessibleRoutes.html	• Surface • Lighting • Width • Grates • Slopes • Protruding Objects • Etc.
Name: **Pedestrian Task Force Committee: Walkability Checklist** *Purpose*: Assess the quality of the walkable environment of certain chosen study areas *Number of questions*: 6 *Assessment area*: Facilities *Manual included*: no *Scoring mechanism*: 1-5 (awful-very good)	Kalamazoo Non-Motorized Transport Plan	• General: Facilities, Safety, Security, Aesthetics, Pleasure, Motorist Behavior, and Access to Transit. • ADA-Related: Curbs, Ramps, Width of Sidewalk, Sidewalk Boundaries, Signals, and Timing of Lights
Name: **Universal Design Audit Checklist** *Purpose*: Assess the design of a facility *Number of questions*: 99 *Assessment area*: Facilities *Manual included*: no *Scoring mechanism*: Score each item with 1, 2, or 3 points	Center for Inclusive Design and Environmental Access www.ap.buffalo.edu/idea or http://www.nyc.gov/html/ddc/pdf/udny/17checklist.pdf	• Access Points • Pathways • Vertical Circulation • Walking Surfaces • Building Features • Amenities

Appendix B: Supplemental Information

TABLE 5: ACCESSIBILITY ASSESSMENTS

Name and Characteristics	Source	Topic Areas
Name: **Access for Disabled People: Access Audit of Sports Facilities** *Purpose*: Assess the design of a sports facility *Number of questions*: 150+ *Assessment area*: Sports facilities *Manual included*: no *Scoring mechanism*: no	Sport England www.sprotengland.org/audit-sheets.pdf	• Arriving at Facility • Emergency Escape • External Features and Ramps • Social Areas • Other Building Specific Features
Name: **Accessing the Arts: Access Audit** *Purpose*: Access of a building *Number of questions*: 108 *Assessment area*: Facilities *Manual included*: no *Scoring mechanism*: no	Accessible Arts www.artsaccessaustralia.org/pdf/audit.pdf	• Accessibility of Public Transport • Wheel Chair Access to Building Including Lights • Colors • Tactile Indicators • Signage
Name: **PBIC Walkability Checklist** *Purpose*: Assess neighbourhood streets *Number of questions*: 5 *Assessment area*: Pedestrian environment *Manual included*: no *Scoring mechanism*: Rate responses on a scale of 1 to 6 and compare to given total scale	Pedestrian and Bicycle Information Center http://www.walkinginfo.org/pdf/walkingchecklist.pdf	• General: Safety, Security, Aesthetics, Pleasure, Motorist Behavior • ADA-Related: Curbs, Size of Sidewalk, General State of Sidewalk, Timing of Lights
Name: **Placecheck** *Purpose*: Assess streets *Number of questions*: 100+ *Assessment area*: Pedestrian environment *Manual included*: no *Scoring mechanism*: no	Placecheck http://placecheck.info/placechecklist_full.htm	• Aesthetics • Functionality • Accessibility of Public Transport • Safety • Security • Landmarks
Name: **Access audit check list** *Purpose*: Accessibility of paths without motorized traffic *Number of questions*: 17 *Assessment area*: Paths without motorized vehicles *Manual included*: no *Scoring mechanism*: no	Sustrans http://www.sustrans.org.uk/webfiles/scottland/ff42-	• Surfaces • Inclines • Barriers • Furniture • Inclines • Signage • Steps • Handrails
Name: **Pedestrian network planning and facilities design guide** *Purpose*: Assess the design of a sports facility *Number of questions*: 150+ *Assessment area*: Sports facilities *Manual included*: no *Scoring mechanism*: no	Land Transport NZ http://www.ltsa.govt.nz/consultation/ped-network-plan/appendix2.html	• Arriving at Facility • Emergency Escape • External Features and Ramps • Social Areas • Other Building Specific Features

TABLE 5: ACCESSIBILITY ASSESSMENTS

Name and Characteristics	Source	Topic Areas
Name: **ADA Review** *Purpose*: Assess safety of an intersection *Number of questions*: 14 criteria *Assessment area*: Intersections *Manual included*: no *Scoring mechanism*: no	Florida DOT, received from Lexington, KY	• Ramps • Slopes • Width • Landings • Push Buttons • Tactile Surface
Name: **Lexington Fayette Pedestrian Facility Inventory** *Purpose*: Assess safety of intersections and crosswalks *Number of questions*: 3 sections *Assessment area*: Intersections and crosswalks *Manual included*: no *Scoring mechanism*: no	Lexington, KY	• Intersection Configuration and Facilities • Signage • Signals • Sidewalk • Ramps • Drains • Trash Receptacles • Speed Limit • Number of Traffic Lanes
Name: **Designing Sidewalks and Trails for Access Part II of II: Best Practices Design Guide** *Purpose*: Provides guidance to planners, designers, and transportation engineers on how to design pedestrian facilities for all users to include those with disabilities. As well as to help develop quantitative assessments of the conformance of the pedestrian facility network to the ADA Guidelines. *Number of questions*: *Assessment area*: Accessible facilities *Manual included*: yes *Scoring mechanism*: no	Federal Highway Administration	• Sidewalks • Curb Ramps • Driveway Crossings • Median Cut-Throughs • Median Ramps • Protruding Objects • Grades • Etc.
Name: **Healthy Aging Research Network Environmental Audit Tool and Protocol** *Purpose*: Quantitative and qualitative assessment of community-scale and street-scale factors associated with physical activity in older adults. *Number of questions*: 13 pages *Assessment area*: Pedestrian environment *Manual included*: no *Scoring mechanism*: no	Healthy Aging Network http://depts.washington.edu/harn	• Types of Land Uses • Construction Activity • Sidewalks • Buffers • Slopes • Maintenance • Obstructions • Street Amenities • Signage • Crosswalks

Appendix B: Supplemental Information